MW00987918

Count the Stars

In the unending drama of today's culture, in the midst of modern life's intimidating contortions, one longs for a voice of hope. Dr Matthew Turner's newest book, *Count the Stars*, is a timely and a readable response, calling us to that place of intimacy with God where we can hear again, believe again and obey without fear. You'll be blessed by this book and I recommend it.

Mark Rutland, PhD, Executive Director, *The National Institute of Christian Leadership*

***

I have been a night-sky lover for a long time. Nothing is more peaceful to me than to look into the star-lit blackened backdrop of a crisp night canopy and be reminded that there is a BIG GOD... and I'm not Him! Dr. Turner's wonderful look into the life of Abraham and God's patient interaction with him could not be a more timely read! The dark skies of uncertainty and difficulty are all around us. But so are the stars! As you dive into Count the Stars, you will be encouraged and transformed... you will also never look into the night sky the same again! Enjoy.

Sam Hemby PhD., Professor of Leadership, *Southeastern University*

***

Dr. Matthew Turner has written a clear, simple, and concise book on how to cut through the clutter and noise to hear the voice of God for your life. This book is a must-read for anyone wanting to experience the awe and wonder of God and to experience his plans and purposes for their lives.

Dr. Eric Speir, Academic Director, *Nelson University*

***

Matthew Turner takes us on an insightful journey with the Biblical patriarch Abraham. You will feel yourself leaving Ur of the Chaldees, struggling with Abraham and Sarah in Egypt, wondering how God will perform His promise of a child born late in life, and looking into the night sky in amazement at the magnitude of God's promises. This is an excellent book for laity and preachers alike as we grow in our walk with the same God who called Abraham four thousand years ago. You will hear that same divine voice calling you to the exciting journey of faith.

Dr. Doug Beacham, General Superintendent, *International Pentecostal Holiness Church*

***

Most pastors and leaders desire to lead their family and friends through a daring journey to a daring destination, but often lack the vehicle to transport them from "the now" to "the next." In his book, *Count the Stars,* my friend, Matthew Turner, has created such a vehicle. By engaging in God's promise to Abram in Genesis 15, you will see how God enters into a sacred cooperation with you in your own spiritual journey. In short, if you really want to explore God's plans and purposes for your life, this is the book for you.

Dr. Wayman Ming Jr., General Bishop, Pentecostal Church of God, *Bedford, Texas*

***

Answering God's call and pursuing God's promise can be daunting, especially if that pilgrimage leads to places of conflict, privation, and physical limitation. But with God as your shield you can proceed with confidence, for He who names and numbers the stars knows your name and the number of steps it will take to lead you from promise to fulfillment. In *Count the Stars,* Dr. Matthew Turner helps us rediscover the rapture of the upward look, enabling us to behold the wonder, majesty, and faithfulness of God.

Dr. Mark L. Williams, Senior Pastor, *North Cleveland Church of God, Cleveland, Tenn.*

***

This is an excellent book. It intrigues me. It is the best book on Abraham that I have ever read. Dr. Turner takes this first real man of scriptural faith and compares His journey to that of today's believer. The comparisons can be phenomenal. Abraham "believed the Lord" and had a miraculous life. So may ever reader of this book as They obey and "believe the Lord".

D. Chris Thompson, President of Holmes Bible College, *Greenville, S.C.*

***

Maybe it was the timing that I read *Count the Stars* that made it so stirring for me…but when is it not a good time to be reminded that God still speaks to His people? As I read through each chapter, my memory was flooded with the times that God has so clearly spoken into my life. Dr Matthew made Abraham's experience with God come alive in my mind's eye as he shared his own personal experiences. What a delight! I feel a renewed desire to step outside, look up into the night sky, and try to *Count the Stars* again!

Pastor Curt Johnson, Senior Co-Pastor, *North Griffin Church, Griffin, GA.*

***

The theme of *Count the Stars* reminds me of the old hymn, 'Count Your Blessings,' as we recall with fondness the many, many times God reaches down to us in our distress and reminds us to name those blessings, 'one by one.' God's promises to us give us the assurance that His blessings and 'stars' are abundant and everlasting.

Bishop Tim Hill, Presiding Bishop, *Church of God, Cleveland, Tennessee*

***

Dr. Turner in his second published book has once again hit a home run. You will be inspired and encouraged by *Count the Stars*. As you read through this book allow yourself to become immersed in the fact that God knows your name and has an incredible plan for your future. If it seems too big or impossible chances are good that it is from God. Yes, He wants to use you with all of your shortcomings to help full-fill his amazing work.

Pastor Billy Smith, Senior Pastor, *Christ Chapel Community Church, Zebulon, GA.*

***

In *Count the Stars,* Dr. Matthew Turner takes a unique approach to a superhero of faith, Abraham, who is called a friend of God and known as the father to the nation of Israel. Matthew looks at the mighty man of faith, Abraham, from his humanity and even his struggles as he hears from God and reveals that even when Abraham showed his humanity the most, God did not change His mind about Abraham. Matthew intertwines personal testimonies throughout the book, showing that we, too, can be like Abraham if we have the faith that Abraham possessed. *Count the Stars* is a beautiful book of encouragement that helps us remember that we have a Father who is a friend and cares for us.

Bishop Scotty Poole, General Superintendent, *Congregational Holiness Church, Griffin, GA.*

COUNT

THE

STARS

BY MATTHEW TURNER

Published by KHARIS PUBLISHING, an imprint of
KHARIS MEDIA LLC.

Copyright © 2024 Matthew Turner

ISBN-13: 978-1-63746-259-1

ISBN-10: 1-63746-259-X

Library of Congress Control Number: 2024939115

All KHARIS PUBLISHING products are available at special
quantity discounts for bulk purchase for sales promotions,
premiums, fund-raising, and educational needs. For details,
contact:

Kharis Media LLC
Tel: 1-630-909-3405
support@kharispublishing.com
www.kharispublishing.com

Contents

To my wife, Anna Kate. You have filled my life with wonder beyond measure.
You have pushed me to new heights in ministry and into deeper revelations in God.
I love you more than the stars in the sky.
Your loving husband.

Acknowledgments

In writing *Count the Stars* I have learned that a project like this draws not only from revelations in Scripture, but also from wonderful relationships with amazing people. The examples and personal stories within this book are based on relationships with which God has richly blessed me, and I am forever grateful.

I dedicated this book to my helpmate, Anna Kate. Our life together has been one grand adventure. You have stood beside me, prayed for me, encouraged me, and pushed me to excel. Thank you for loving me the way you do, and I thank God for joining my life to yours.

Holmes Bible College and former College President Chris Thompson, hold a special place in my heart. While I never attended HBC, I became an author there. It was while speaking to the faculty and staff that God spoke to me, telling me to write. The result was my first book, *Follow Him*. It was that first step that led to *Count The Stars*. I am forever grateful for the amazing institution of Holmes Bible College and for my friendship with President Thompson.

God blessed my family and I more than I can put into words for the friendship of pastors Curt and Beth

Johnson of the North Griffin Congregational Holiness Church. They are two of the most anointed people I know. Their ministry has poured into my family and has challenged us to go deeper in God. This book and its focus came from sitting in the pews of the North Griffin Church. Thank you, Pastors Curt, and Beth, for everything!

I beam with such pride over my three children, Elia Kate, Edyth Ray, and Ephraim Franklin, who fill me with joy and wonder every single day. No matter what type of day I've had, their loving and smiling faces fill me with gratitude. I work every day to be a loving father to those three miracles.

Finally, I am extremely grateful for the editorial team and staff at Kharis Publishing who took a chance on me to publish this work. My life intersecting with this amazing and godly company was nothing short of the work of a Master Designer. Thank you, Kharis, for all you have done for me and for *Count The Stars*!

Introduction

Have you ever heard a song, and it seemed every word, every stanza, even the musical notes were written specifically for you, and you burst into tears, realizing it was no coincidence you were hearing that song at that very moment? As you listened to the song, you felt the presence of God, as if He were standing in front of you, wrapping His arms around you, immediately filling you with peace, love, and abounding joy. The moment was so powerful that you have never forgotten it, and you are most likely replaying the moment in your mind now. Like you, I have had a moment just like this, and I will never forget it, either.

The year 2007 was one of dynamic change in my life. Graduating high school and entering college is an important and scary time for anyone, and it was for me, too. I began college two months after graduating high school, and God opened the door for me to serve in my first leadership role in the Church. I was asked to come to the Centre Congregational Holiness Church and serve as the youth pastor. I was beyond excited about this opportunity. I knew immediately the opportunity was God's will for my life, and I enthusiastically accepted the position. Very quickly, though, the stress and understanding of all the moving pieces in my life began to overwhelm me. *What is college going to be like? What will be my choice of a degree? Am I ready to lead teenagers while I am still a teenager myself? What if I fail? Fail college? Fail the students who have been entrusted to me?* I kept all of this to myself and told no one.

It was during this time when I was having something of a spiritual and emotional crisis that I also was helping with music at our annual youth camp. The director brought a song I had not previously heard for the youth choir to sing, although the song had been released two years prior. As soon as I heard the first line, the Spirit of the Lord grabbed my attention. I immediately knew God wanted to use this song to speak to me. How did I know? While it is hard to describe the cognitive reasoning that brings one to the understanding that the Creator is speaking, Jesus answered this question rather simply: "My sheep hear My voice, and I know them, and they follow Me" (Jn. 10:27). I heard His voice and I felt His presence as the notes rang out on the piano and our choir director began to sing it for the first time:

He counts the stars one and all

He knows how much sand is on the shores

He sees every sparrow that falls

He made the mountains and the seas

He's in control of everything

Of all creatures great and small

And He knows my name

Every step that I take

Every move that I make

Every tear that I cry

He knows my name

When I'm overwhelmed by the pain

And can't see the light of day

I know I'll be just fine

'Cause He knows my name

I don't know what tomorrow will bring

I can't tell you what's in store

I don't know a lot of things

I don't have all the answers

To the questions of my life

But I know in Whom I have believed[1]

To me, it was as if God pulled up a chair where I was sitting, looked me in the eye, and assured me that everything was going to be ok. As the song mentions, the feeling I had was not from empty words or catchy "Christianese" that we often hear or say. His words were filled with proof. They caused me to stop thinking about all the issues that were swirling around me, and to place my eyes and mind on the One who created all things and who holds all things in His hands. Job said, "In whose hand is the life of every living thing and the

---

[1] *He Knows my Name©*, 2013, Annie and Kelly McRae, Gospel Lighthouse

breath of all mankind?" (Job 12:10). As I moved my focus off my problems and placed it on God, who He is, and all He has done, several things happened. First, the weight of the world that I was carrying began to lift as I became filled with the *wonder* and *majesty* of God. Second, a great peace settled down in my spirit, assuring me that while I did not know the answers to all the questions I previously listed, God did, and He was and is with me. Last, I was reminded that my future and what God wanted for my life had already been beautifully planned. I was filled with amazement as the weight of all the fear and worry began to lift off my chest. I remembered that God holds my whole life in the palms of His hands. I was filled with *awe* and *wonder* as I thought about how God loved me, desired good for my life, and had been and would continue to be with me all the days of my life.

In Genesis 15, Abram also found himself overwhelmed with the anxiety of life. In fact, Abram's anxiety was so bad that when God came to him, Abram could not hear or accept anything God had to say. He was so overwhelmed with his own issues that all he could focus on was the mountain of a problem in front of him. Just look at the response that Abram gave the Lord after God greeted him and said He desired to bless Abram. "Lord God, what will You give me, seeing I go childless, and the heir of my house *is* Eliezer of Damascus?" Then Abram said, "Look, You have given me no offspring; indeed one born in my house is my heir!" (Gen. 15:2-3). The Lord came to Abram desiring to bless him, but Abram was so consumed by his disappointment and his fear of living his whole life without having a son that he could not receive a wonderful greeting from the Lord.

I love how open and honest Abram was with God. Even more, I love how the Lord did not shun Abram for being so open and honest. Abram learned that God not only understood where Abram was and what he felt, but also that God was about to forever change his life. The Lord invited Abram to take his eyes and focus off the problem he was facing and to look up into the night sky and view the stars. The Lord wanted to melt the worry off Abram's shoulders and to cause him to be filled with wonder and hope. The Lord said to Abram, "Look now toward heaven, and count the stars if you are able to number them." (Gen. 15:5). In other words, the Lord told Abram to look up and see all that I have done in the heavens. If I have done all of this then I can also work a miracle in your life and give you what your heart desires the most

Fear and anxiety are not new experiences for me or you. There have been many moments, days, or longer seasons when we have been assaulted by these tools of Satan. According to the Anxiety and Depression Association of America®, "…anxiety disorders are the most common mental illness in the US affecting 40 million adults ages 18 and older every year."[2] Scripture

---

[2] https://adaa.org/understanding-anxiety/facts-statistics accessed 3/14/2024

declares God's will for the lives of people around the world and it is not to be filled with fear and anxiety. Rather, God's great will is for His people to be filled with power, love, and a sound mind. This does not mean that a follower of Christ does not have moments of fear and anxiety, however, your life and mine do not have to be consumed with worry. Jesus' death on the cross and victory from the grave have once and for all provided the victory over death, hell, the grave, and even Satan himself. If you know Christ as your Savior, then Scripture declares in Ephesians 3:17 that He that is within you; He is greater than Satan who is in the world (1 John 4:4). Fear, worry, and anxiety have been defeated and you do not have to live chained to them. You can walk in freedom today. The very first step is to know Jesus as your Savior and King.

Perhaps you picked up this book because it was a gift, or maybe something about the title or cover intrigued you, but if you are reading this introduction and you have never given your heart to Jesus Christ, I believe your interaction with this book has taken place by Divine Providence. God loves you and desires you to come into a relationship with Him, and for you to walk with God and God with you in a relationship, you must first ask God to forgive you of your sins. I know there are some wonderful people in this world who feel like they are good people both morally and in their actions. Scripture declares, "…for all have sinned and fall short of the glory of God…" (Rom. 3:23). Since we all have sin in our lives and there is no amount of good deeds that we could perform to rid our lives of sin, we need a Savior to do what we cannot. The Bible shares, "For God so loved the world that He gave His only begotten Son, that whoever believes in Him should not perish but have everlasting life. For God did not send His Son into the world to condemn the world, but that the world through Him might be saved" (John 3:16-17) God so loved you that He has provided a way for us to be in relationship with Him at His own expense. Paul also shares the precise way that one can receive Christ as Savior and how sin can be forever washed out of your life. "If you confess with your mouth the Lord Jesus and believe in your heart that God has raised Him from the dead, you will be saved" (Rom. 10:9). Today can be the day that you receive Christ as your Savior by acknowledging that you have sinned and you confess Christ is Lord. You must believe that Jesus died for the sins in your life and that He was raised from the grave. In so doing you admit that you need Christ to do what you cannot do, and you recognize that He is Lord of your life and of the whole world. As a result, like a loving Father, God forgives you of your sin, welcomes you into a loving relationship, and completely changes your life. You are one prayer away from a new life and a new direction. If you are ready for God to forgive you, and if you are ready to live for Him, I invite you to pray along with me today. Make this your prayer:

Heavenly Father, I know that I am a sinner. I realize I need Jesus to save me from all my sin. Today, I ask you to wash all my sins away. I declare you Lord and

Introduction

Savior of my life. Thank you for coming to this world, dying for my sin, and being raised in victory so I can live in victory with You. I pray You help me to live my life totally and completely for You. Help me to live courageously and boldly for You all the days of my life.

In Jesus name, I pray.

Amen.

The Lord desires your life to be filled with the great *wonder* of *Him* and not the burdens of this world. He desires for you to rest in the fact that He is in control of all things, that in the palm of His hands is your life and every life of every person. And as a master orchestrator, He works on your behalf so that your life is filled with blessings and good. He is in control so you do not have to be filled with the fear and anxiety the enemy tries to use to weigh down your life. This is the message that God began to share with Abram in Genesis chapter fifteen.

When Abram speaks, you immediately recognize that he is so burdened with fear and anxiety that he cannot even receive the great revelation God came to him to share. Thankfully, God understood why Abram felt this way, and He was not mad or offended by Abram's anxiety. God addressed Abram and his fears, and invited him to take his attention off what he felt was going wrong in his life, and focus his attention on the One who placed the stars in the sky and knows them all by name. Abram was human, just like you and me. We can look at his interaction with God and relate to Abram on many levels. Most of all, we can read the story of Abram and learn, as he did, that God is able to do anything in our lives. Since He created and placed the stars in the night sky, surely He can and will care for you.

Let me invite you to turn the page and walk with me as we look at Abram, his family, and the situation surrounding them as God challenged Abram to look to the heavens and *Count the Stars*. God's challenge for Abram was impossible, but it was not so much about counting the stars as it was about getting Abram to lift up his head and cast his eyes upon the One who loved him, and to know God was right there with him. When you know God is with you, working on your behalf, and empowering you, fear and anxiety cannot abide.

Introduction - A Deeper Look

Is there a song that shares the truth of God's love for humanity and has challenged you in your walk? What song is it and what is it about that song that brings encouragement to you?

_____

_____

_____

_____

_____

Are there any issues you constantly deal with that bring fear and anxiety? What are those areas or issues that you need the Lord to bring healing to?

_____

_____

_____

_____

_____

Chapter 1

Unlikely Abram

"After these things the word of the Lord came to Abram in a vision..."

(Gen. 15 :1, emphasis added)

The story of Abram is one of incredible adventure, devastating heartache, and supernatural miracles. It is a true story everyone can look to for both encouragement and conviction. Abram came from a family of polytheistic worshipers, and although he made some extremely terrible decisions in his walk with God, Abram is called a friend of God in both the Old and New Testaments. Abram married a beautiful woman named Sarai. At one point in their journey, Sarai caught the attention of the Pharaoh of Egypt and Abimelech, King of Gerar, and this placed Abram and Sarai in a dangerous position that required them to be apart. However, through divine intervention, God reunited them.

Unlikely Abram

Between two dramatic encounters with Abram and God in Genesis fifteen and seventeen, Moses recorded the uncomfortable incident between Sari, Abram, and Hagar. Out of the deep desire for a child and to see her husband have the heir he so longed for, Sarai convinced Abram to have an intimate relationship with her handmaiden, Hagar. The result of the relationship was a son, Ishmael (Gen 16:16). Abram was eighty-six years old when Ishmael was born. Thirteen years later, and in a supernatural encounter, God made a covenant with Abram and changed his name to Abraham, meaning "father of many nations" and changed Sarai's name to Sarah meaning "princess". Then, when Abram was one hundred years old and Sarah ninety years old, the promised son, Isaac, was born.

Abram was a great leader in many ways. He was a leader of men who, at times, led campaigns like a military superior would. In fact, it is through the journey of Abram that the first war is recorded in Scripture.

Abram loved his wife, sons, and those of his household fiercely. What is evident throughout his story is the high moral character that seemed to shine almost everywhere Abram went. Although Abram did not hail from a great lineage of God followers, when God called out to Abram, he chased after God's call with great passion and purpose.

At the age of 175, Abram died, "...in a good old age, an old man and full *of years*" (Gen. 25:8). His example of faith and covenant with God lived on throughout Scripture, as he is mentioned over 230 times after his death. Still today we are looking at Abram and learning from the blueprint of his life.

Unlikely Abram

After the Tower of Babel in Genesis 11, we learn of the descendants of Noah's son, Shem. From the seed of Shem, Tereh was born, who became the father of Abram. Scripture describes that the native land of both Abram and Tereh as a place called Ur of the Chaldeans (Gen 11:28). This bustling metropolis was located, most scholars believe, in the southern area of modern-day Iraq.[3] In a brief but revealing scripture, Joshua shares that Abram's father, and most likely many others, worshiped idols (Josh. 24:2).

While Ur was a polytheistic society, one particular deity was worshiped above others. The moon goddess was known by many names, two of which were Ningal and Nina. The capital of Babylon, Nineveh, derived its name from this goddess.[4] According to those who relayed the goddess' teaching, deviant sexual rituals were required to bring honor to the idol. The temples of Ningal/Nina were filled with priestesses whose only

---

[3] Blenkinsopp, Joseph. 2016. "The First Family: Terah and Sons." *Journal for the Study of the Old Testament* 41 (1): 3–13. https://search-ebscohost-com.seu.idm.oclc.org/login.aspx?direct=true&db=oah&AN=OTA0000067293&site=eds-live&scope=site.
[4] Henry Halley. Halley's Bible Handbook. (Grand Rapids: Zondervan, 1965) 95.

job was to practice sexual ceremonies with those who came to the temple to worship.[5] The land from which Abram hailed was full of wickedness and perversion, however, this type of perversion was seen in many places prior to Abram; this was nothing new.

The Tower of Babel was a perversion of the intellect and wisdom God gave to man. The Cain's murder of his brother Abel was a perversion of the family and God's design. And despite this long history of sin and perversion, God reached down in the life of one man, Abram. How incredible it is that out of a land of idol worshipers God chose the one person who would be the founder of the Jewish nation.

Suppose for a moment that you were chosen by God to search the whole earth and find the one person who would usher in the next great people through whom God would do amazing wonders. How would you—or should I say *where* would you—begin your search? What kind of family history or heritage would you look for if you were searching for someone who, for thousands of years, would be called "a friend of God"? If I had the task, I absolutely would not search for the "one" in the middle of a polytheistic culture. Abram was an unlikely choice from every viewpoint but God's, and, beloved, you and I are just as unlikely, but God also has chosen you and me.

---

[5] Ibid.

Herein lies one of the most beautiful attributes of our Heavenly Father. He does not think or act the way we think and act. The Lord declared, "'For My thoughts are not your thoughts, Nor are your ways My ways,' says the Lord" (Is. 55:8). There are many examples of how God works in unlikely ways and how He seems to love to choose unlikely people to do His will.

In the book of Judges, God picks a self-admitted weakling to lead a whittled down army to defeat a massive military force made up of several allied nations. Gideon said, "…but how can I save Israel? My clan is the weakest in Manasseh, and I am the least in my family" (Jud. 6:15). God instructs and guides Gideon on exactly how to defeat the enemy and Gideon does so incredibly. In our eyes, was Gideon an unlikely person for God to use? Yes! In the eyes of the Lord, Gideon was perfect for the task at hand. With Gideon, the Lord proved that being physically weak did not disqualify one from being used by Him.

Another very unlikely person whom God used to do amazing feats was David. When the prophet Samuel arrived at Jesse's home to anoint the next king of Israel, David's father did not consider David even worthy enough to be presented before Samuel, much less to be Israel's next king. As the sons of Jesse were presented before Samuel, there were some who seemed like a perfect fit. Whatever the perceived physical attributes of a good king were, Samuel thought he had found the one in Eliab. Samuel even said, "Surely the Lord's anointed *is* before Him!" (1 Sam. 16:6). When God heard that Samuel said this, either aloud or within himself, God spoke! "Do not look at his appearance or at his physical stature, because I have refused him. For *the Lord does* not *see* as man sees; for man looks at the outward appearance, but the Lord looks at the heart" (1 Sam. 16:7). After Samuel had seen all the young men whom Jesse arranged to be presented, the prophet asked if there was anyone else. God's sending Samuel to Jesse's house meant that someone within his house was the chosen one.

God does not send people on assignments to waste time. *If God sent you, there is a purpose.* Jesse politely told Samuel, indeed there was one more son, but he was out keeping sheep (1 Sam. 16:11). When David arrived back at his father's house, his physical appearance was so striking that it is recorded in Scripture. Samuel said, "Now he *was* ruddy, with bright eyes, and good-looking" (1 Sam 16:12). David was youthful in appearance, healthy, and handsome. The Lord spoke to Samuel once again and said, "Arise, anoint him; for this *is* the one!" (1 Sam. 16:12). Although he was dismissed by his family, David was just the man God was looking for. At this moment, God proved that one's age did not disqualify a person from being used by Him.

One last example, although there are many more, of God using the unlikely to do amazing things in the Kingdom is found in the New Testament. The Apostle Paul was an incredible leader in the early church and wrote two-thirds of the 27 books in the New

Testament. However, before Paul was Paul, he was a ruthless hunter of Christians named Saul. Luke said of Saul's activities, "As for Saul, he made havoc of the church, entering every house, and dragging off men and women, committing *them* to prison" (Acts 8:3, emphasis added). Before Christ, Saul was a madman who believed his cause was absolute. Not only had he put many in prison, but he also approved of some being killed simply because they were Christians. Despite how unlikely Saul's choices made him, God looked upon the heart of Saul and saw great potential. When God changed Saul's life, he became Paul, the apostle who arguably did more for the early church than any other person.

All of these men previously mentioned are just a handful of the examples in Scripture of God using people who were unlikely characters. Abram, too, was an unlikely person to be used by God, but being unlikely was not a disqualifier. In fact, as we will discuss, God loves to use people who are unlikely so the world might also witness His great power. No matter how you may feel about yourself, your past, or your prospects for your future, *you* are the very type of person God desires to use.

Unreliable Abram

"Now there was a famine in the land, and Abram went down to Egypt to dwell there, for the famine *was* severe in the land" (Genesis 12:10, emphasis added). It is not hard to understand why Abram made the decision to take a detour from the path God had spoken to him about and travel southward to Egypt. Even though Scripture says the famine in the land was severe, the Lord never intended Abram and Sarai to journey south to Egypt. Scripture gives away the outcome before Abram and Sarai arrive in Egypt. The Bible says, "Abram went DOWN to Egypt." Indeed, they went down. Their troubles only multiplied when Abram and Sarai decided it would be better to tell a half-truth about their marriage.

The decisions of Abram in this part of his story are hard to read. After having such a supernatural encounter with the God of heaven, and trusting Him to leave the land, family, and community he knew, Abram began to rely on himself rather than the Lord. As the two make it into Egypt, Abram devised a plan to tell the leaders of Egypt that Sarai was his sister rather than his wife. This wasn't exactly an outright lie. Sarai was indeed Abram's half-sister (Gen. 20:12). However, Abram chose to conceal the whole truth of Sarai being his wife. He did this because he was afraid for his life. Sarai was beautiful and one of the social norms of the day was that when a new family group came into a land or new culture, if men wanted the woman of that family group, they would kill the husband so the woman would be free to marry again. It sounds crazy in our day, but for Abram it was a very real threat.

Upon entering Egypt, just as Abram feared, the "princes of Pharaoh also saw her and commended her to Pharaoh. And the woman was taken to Pharaoh's house" (Gen. 12:15). Can you imagine what this must have been like for Abram? The fear of what was happening to his wife must have been almost unbearable. Can you imagine what it must have been like for Sarai? The fear of the unknown must have been palpable. However, in their minds, Abram and Sarai had to keep up the ruse. Pharaoh, thinking Sarai was only Abram's sister, rewarded Abram with much wealth, giving him sheep, oxen, donkeys, camels, and servants as gifts for bringing Sarai into Egypt (Gen. 12:16). However, the troubles were only just beginning for Pharaoh and his household; because Pharaoh took Sarai, God sent "great plagues" upon his household.

This is so interesting because it is the first time God's punishment is seen upon those who came against Abram. For the Lord told Abram, "I will bless those who bless you, And I will curse him who curses you" (Gen 12:2-3). How incredible! God intervened on behalf of Abram and his family simply because He said He would protect them. God will never lie and He will perform that which He said He would do. Pharaoh quickly learned that Sarai was not only Abram's sister, but in fact his wife. The leader of Egypt told Abram and Sarai, to take all the livestock and goods and to get out of the country. Despite the terrible leadership that Abram displayed in this moment in his life, God blessed him and his family tremendously upon their exit from Egypt. You would think such trouble would have taught Abram to never lie about the truth of his marriage, but in Genesis 20, Abram once again lied about the true identity of his wife.

A Moment of Wonder

"Wow! Look at the stars!" This was how my oldest daughter grabbed my attention one cool clear night. I was busy trying to get my family of five out of the car, along with all of the bags that are needed to travel with three kids. My mind was not on gazing into the heavens but rather on trying to get everyone inside so my wife and I could work on getting the kids in bed. When my oldest got my attention, I stopped and looked up into the night sky, and beaming back at me was the light from an innumerable sea of stars. It was so clear that, for the first time in my life, I saw what I believed to be one of the spiral arms of the Milky Way galaxy. I was taken aback by the massive size, the beautiful colors, and I began to think about how, with mere words, God spoke all that I saw in the sky that night into existence. We stood in awe, wonder, and silence as we looked up into the heavens and stared at the grandeur of all the stars in the night sky. With the same type of wonder, I stand in awe of God's incredible love for me and you.

Despite understanding Abram's background and some of his unbelievable decisions, God chose him and used him to give birth to a nation that would be God's own special people. This very fact causes me to stop and be in awe of our God. Did God know that Abram came from a people who served all types of idols? Did God understand that the type of "worship" the people of Ur were involved in was all manner of debauchery and sexual promiscuity? Yes, He did. God knew all of this and more. Also, despite Abram's repeated choices of lying and deception, we never find God deciding that He'd had enough of Abram. In fact, you never hear that God changed His mind in the least bit about choosing to love Abram and to use him to father the Jewish nation. Here is our moment of wonder: God knows everything about our lives. He knows our past, our failures, and mistakes. Yet, when God sees us He is filled with love and compassion for us. His love does not come from some sense of duty or responsibility. His love does not come from our decisions and our actions. *God loves you simply because He does.* There are no words that could adequately describe the depths of His love; there are no words that could describe why God loves us the way He does. He loves us because He *is* love and has decided to love us no matter what.

I am convinced there are things about God that you cannot grasp until you become a parent. I have a seven-year-old, and I suppose every parent feels this way, but she is crazy smart for her age. She understands concepts at seven that I don't think I understood until my early teens. Recently, I was talking to her about how much God loves her. The conversation moved into explaining why God loves her, me, her mom, her siblings, and everyone in the world. I came to a place where I had to stop talking and think for a moment. *How can I explain this so my seven-year-old can understand?* But then I thought, *I don't even fully understand why God loves us. As often as we fail Him, after all the terrible mistakes, after what I did yesterday, after I said those terrible things, why does God love me?*

He loves because He does. While you can decide to no longer love God, serve Him, or live for Him; God will never stop loving you. John said it like this, "We love Him because He first loved us" (1 Jn. 4:19). When His love started we do not know; I think He has always loved you and me. His love is unreasonable because there is nothing we can do to make His love disappear. It is unending because in all our days on earth, there will never be a day when we do not live under and in the mighty love of God. His love is unchanging because He has never changed His mind, nor will He change His mind about us. His love is uncomplicated because there is nothing we can do to "earn" His love. We have His love because He has given it to us. Finally, it is unconditional because there is nothing that can separate us from His great love (Rom. 8:38).

I look at the life of Abram and I am reminded of how God loves me. I see how there was nothing that changed God's mind about Abram, and I am encouraged that the way God loved Abram is the same way He loves me. As a result, I stand in wonder of God's amazing love. If you have not been told today, I'll tell you now: God loves you so much, no matter what.

Chapter 1 - A Deeper Look

Seeing how Abram struggled with the same types of things so many of us do today, how does this encourage you in your walk with God?

_____

_____

_____

_____

_____

How does God's unfailing love for you affect your life?

_____

_____

_____

_____

_____

_____

Have you ever questioned why the Lord led you to the place you have served in the past or maybe where you are now? How has the Lord encouraged you?

_____

_____

_____

_____

_____

_____

Have you ever tried to figure out a situation without praying about it and asking the Lord for wisdom? How did it work for you?

_____

_____

_____

_____

_____

_____

_____

Chapter 2

God Speaks to Abram

"After these things the word of the Lord came to Abram in a vision..."

(Gen. 15:1, emphasis added).

Have you ever heard the voice of God? Has the Lord ever spoken to you? If you have made Christ your Savior, then you have had the Lord speak to you at least once. Jesus told us, "No one can come to Me unless the Father who sent Me draws him; and I will raise him up at the last day" (John 6:44). Therefore, whatever your salvation experience was like, it was the Father who drew you to Christ. How did He draw you? God, in His amazing grace and kindness, spoke from Heaven through time and space directly to your heart and let you know that He loved you and desired a relationship with you. After you heard or felt the voice of God speak to you, you responded to His voice by asking Him to forgive you and be Lord of your life.

God Speaks to Abram

If you have made Christ your Savior, then I believe you have heard the voice of God on numerous occasions. As Scripture displays, God desires to speak to His beloved sons and daughters. In fact, the Old Testament alone records over 2,000 times when God spoke to His people. God's desire to speak to His people is not limited only to the pages of our Bibles. While there is no doubt that one way God speaks is through His Word, He also still speaks, guides, and directs us in direct communication from His mouth to our spiritual ears.

Imagine for a moment needing an answer from the Lord about your life, or a situation you are facing that has caused you great grief. You go to God in prayer, the Father hears your petition, and while He knows exactly what the answer is for your situation, instead of speaking to you, He covers His mouth and refuses to answer. That is the definition of cruelty in my mind.

I will be honest, if I could not hear from the Lord, I am not sure I would be a Christian today. Again, it was His voice, His calling, that drew me to a place of repentance. While there are those within Christianity who believe and teach that God speaking to us today is folly, beloved, I want to encourage you that God has not changed. The God of the Bible is still alive and well today, and He is still speaking. You are not alone in your walk with God. You do not have to figure out this life on your own, for you have a friend closer than your own sibling who desires to lead and guide you. If we believe the Bible, which says, "Jesus Christ the same yesterday, and today, and forever" (Heb. 13:8); if we are going to believe the Lord which said, "For I am the Lord God and I change not" (Malachi 3:6), then, beloved, we must also believe that God's desire is to speak to us today.

God Speaks to Abram

A great deal has occurred in the life of Abram in just three chapters leading up to chapter fifteen of Genesis. Moses, the writer of Genesis, calls our attention to the moment God spoke to Abram in a vision. "After these things the word of the Lord came to Abram in a vision, saying, "Do not be afraid, Abram. I *am* your shield, your exceedingly great reward" (Gen. 15:1). This is not the first time that God has spoken to Abram. Still, it's hard to know exactly when God first spoke to Abram. I say it is hard to know because some scholars say that God first spoke when Abram's father, Terah, decided to leave Ur in Genesis eleven. Scripture says, "And Terah took his son Abram and his grandson Lot, the son of Haran, and his daughter-in-law Sarai, his son Abram's wife, and they went out with them from Ur of the Chaldeans to go to the land of Canaan; and they came to Haran and dwelt there" (Gen. 11:31). We are not told that God spoke, but the fact that Terah and his family decided to leave makes me wonder why Terah made such a decision to leave the metropolitan city of Ur for the wilderness. Whether or not God spoke to Terah or Abram in Genesis eleven I cannot say for certain, but we do know that God spoke in Genesis 12:1. The Lord said, "Now the Lord had said to Abram: "Get out of your country, From your family and from your father's house to a land that I will show you."

How wonderful it is to hear the voice of God. How wonderful it is that God desires to speak to His children. When I hear God's voice, there are so many thoughts that occur to me. It is a jolting moment when you hear God's voice as you recognize that the Creator of the universe is speaking. I also am overwhelmed with the thought that while God is omnipresent, He is everywhere at every moment, He had a message to speak to me in a particular moment of time when I needed to hear. No doubt this was what occurred in Gen. 12:1. At the perfect moment and time when Abram needed to hear from God, He spoke. God's message to Abram was simple: get out and get to. God spoke and told Abram to get out of the country where he currently lived and get to a place that God prepared for him and his coming descendants. Notice that God did not call Abram to get out of the country he was in until God also had a place for Abram to get into.

Beloved, God will never call you out of something without knowing where He is taking you.

While it may not be immediately known to you, God has a next step, a next place for you; God does not leave things to chance. God does not say, "Let's see what happens." God has a plan for your life, just as He had a plan for Abram. God often does not reveal all His plan to those He speaks to from the beginning, but do not mistake God's silence about the full plan for your life to mean that God does not care. God desires us to trust His voice when He speaks, and as we take a step, He will reveal the next step.

I will never forget when God called me away from a "land" I knew where I was very comfortable. While God's voice was clear about leaving, I was not sure of my next step for some time. I was pastoring and had been for the previous eight years in Alabama. My wife and I loved where we were. Those eight years of pastoring were also our first eight years of marriage, as I became pastor just three months after our wedding, but God's voice was so clear, *it's time to leave Piedmont.* I understood God's voice so clearly that I turned in my resignation the next Sunday. To make matters even more unnerving, we lived in the church parsonage. While I am sure the wonderful people of the church would have allowed us to stay longer, we knew to honor the church correctly we needed to be completely out of the house by my last Sunday. Leaving the church meant we had no place to live. We obviously had many questions; where we were going to live being the greatest of the questions. While we should have been filled with all types of anxiety for the future, instead we were filled with a great sense of wonder and adventure. Many around us thought we had lost our minds. Our parents were very worried about us, and understandably so, but we knew God said, *it's time to leave Piedmont.* Weeks passed, and then a phone call came from a denominational leader who told us of an opportunity to work for the denomination my wife and I both grew up attending. Then the Lord spoke again, *this is your next step*. To say that everything fell into place would be too simple. God supernaturally worked step after step for us not only to accept the position, but also to be confirmed by the leadership, move into the home provided for the position, receive the finances needed to move, and countless other things.

As you read the account of Abram's life from Genesis twelve on, you see that God worked out so many steps for him and his family as well. Once again, this is how God works. He will never call us out without having our next step planned. Did God not say, "'I will go before you and make the crooked places straight...'" (Is. 45:2)? Be encouraged today that God is working on your behalf. He is working in your "now," helping you and blessing you, but also God is working in your future, preparing a path, your next place.

Jesus also spoke of preparing a place for us. "I go to prepare a place for you. And if I go and prepare a place for you, I will come again and receive you to Myself; that where I am, *there* you may be also" (John. 14:2-3). One day, Christ is coming back for us, but He first is preparing our next place for us. Once our next place is prepared, He will return and call us home. Once your next place is prepared, and the timing is right in His time, God will call you out of where you are and into your next place.

What Does God's Voice Sound Like?

I love watching the nature documentaries that National Geographic™ or BBC™ produces. I love learning about nature and animals, but I think the main reason I love those types of shows is because the narrator always has the most calming voice. It's the voice of David Attenborough, or Morgan Freeman, or voices like theirs that often are featured. Their voices are so unique and calming. I think people often wonder if God's voice will sound something like a voice they have heard before. So we ask the question: what does God's voice sound like?

When God spoke to Abram, I wonder how he would have described God's voice? Could he describe it? Could he put the right words together to adequately describe the Creator's voice? What about you? Could you describe what you have heard from the Lord? Truthfully, only you will be able to answer the question of God's voice. While someone might do a good job describing it, one must hear Him to fully understand. I think we can look at Scripture and look at our own lives to help us understand what God's voice sounds like, at least in part.

What God's voice sounds like is a question I have been asked many times, especially when I pastored, but it always has been asked in a different way. A great deal of the time, the question was posed as: "How do I know that God is speaking to me?" That question is one everyone asks, whether we voice the question to someone else or not. Is this God speaking? Did I hear the voice of the Lord? It was a question that Samuel asked in Scripture as well. However, when Samuel first heard the voice of the Lord, he initially thought it was the voice of his mentor, Eli. This is because he had no previous encounter with the voice of God. It was the first time that God called to young Samuel. Three different times God called to Samuel and the young boy went to Eli and said, *I heard you call, what can I do for you?* The last time Samuel went to Eli, the prophet, well advanced in years, perceived that Samuel was hearing from the Lord. Eli gave a piece of wisdom to Samuel that I believe forever changed Samuel's life and also can impact your life today.

Eli told Samuel, "Go, lie down: and it shall be, if He calls you, that you must say, 'Speak, Lord, for your servant hears'" (1 Samuel 3:9). First, as Samuel laid back down, there is no doubt he was expecting God to speak to him again. As we have previously discussed, God wants to speak to you. You should also expect God to speak. If you are expecting God to speak you, you will be alert to His voice. While Scripture does not say, I highly doubt that Samuel went back to sleep as he laid down awaiting God to speak once more. I am sure his excitement prevented him from sleeping. However, when God spoke, Samuel was ready to receive.

Now, of course I don't mean we should not get some sleep, but I do believe that we should be open for God to speak to us anytime. Perhaps you are in a drive-through getting your favorite coffee, and God speaks to you about paying for the person behind you. Or perhaps you are in the grocery store and the Lord pricks your heart about sharing your faith with someone that you passed on aisle seven. Pick up your Bible and expect God to speak to you, turn on your Christian radio station and expect God to speak. Wake up every day knowing that today God wants to speak and be ready to hear. Samuel learned to expect to hear God's voice.

Lastly, Eli told Samuel to respond to God's voice. One of the most wonderful truths about our Father is that He wants to have a conversation with us. God does not just want to bark out commands and instructions like some mad drill sergeant. No, God wants to hear from us as much as He desires to speak to us. God told the prophet Jeremiah, "Call to Me, and I will answer you, and show you great and mighty things, which you do not know" (Jer. 33:3). God longs to hear your voice. He longs to hear what is on your mind and what is concerning you. Today—right now even—if you have not spoken to the Lord today, or maybe you cannot remember the last time you spoke to your Heavenly Father, let me encourage you to talk to God. Open up to the One who loves you. We call it prayer, but prayer is simply a communication with God. Call on Him and then listen.

God Speaks to Abram

For Abram, God's Voice was Distinguishable

During the course of one day, how many people do you speak to? How many voices do you hear? Could it be four or five? Or is it higher, say ten to fifteen? I know there are many factors that go into determining that number for you. I have thought about this and I average speaking to seven people a day. Obviously, there are days where that number is much higher because of the settings or services I attend. However, no matter how high your number may be, I am sure you would say, like me, that when God speaks to you it is totally different than anyone else's voice. His voice is distinguishable in my life. I believe this was true for Abram, as well.

In Genesis 12, 13, 15, and every time God spoke to Abram, we never read that Abram wondered within himself, *is that God speaking to me?* We never read that Abram had to fast and pray to see if it was the Lord who gave him the commands and guidance for his life. Abram just knew God's voice.

Jesus said it like this, "My sheep hear my voice, and I know them, and they follow me" (Jn. 10:27). Why would God's people, the sheep Jesus spoke of, follow Christ when they hear His voice? It is because when Jesus speaks there is something within us that tells us this is not the voice of just anyone, but **our Spirit recognizes its Creator and we know, it's Him.** God's voice is distinct.

For Abram, God's Voice was Understandable

When I think back over my life and the times when I heard the voice of the Lord, there was never a time when I did not understand what God said. Now, that doesn't mean I did not have any questions; I most certainly did, but I understood what He said completely. When God told me it was time to leave the church I was pastoring, as I told you previously, there was never a question in my mind about what God said. I heard clearly and understood completely.

I believe it was very much the same for Abram. From the first moment that God spoke and told him to leave the place and people he was comfortable living amongst, while Abram certainly did not know what the end destination would be, he knew God clearly spoke to him to leave. The actions of Abram testify that he understood what God said to him. After God spoke to Abram in Genesis 12 about leaving his country and countrymen, the next verse says, "…so Abram departed as the Lord had spoken to him…" (Gen. 12:4). There was no question in Abram's mind what God spoke to him, and you will also understand Him when God speaks to you.

A Moment of Wonder

Understanding that God desires to speak to us, and when He does, we will be able to distinguish and understand His voice, brings up one more question in our minds: What will God say to me? How exciting and how wonderful it is to think about what God might say to us. Thinking about what God might say to me and you truly is a thing of great wonder.

My wife and I have done this often in our almost fifteen years of marriage. A conversation will somehow be started about our future. We will talk about where we think we might be in ten or twenty years. We start throwing out ideas of what we would like to do and what we would love to be able to do in ministry. No matter what the specifics are about our conversation, it is always predicated on whatever the Lord may speak to us about. While we may say we would love to move closer to family, have a working farm, be surrounded by nature and beauty, if that is not what God calls us to do, then we don't want that, no matter how nice it may sound. Our greatest desire is to be in the will of God. So if God calls us to leave our comfort zone, like He did Abram, then with the Lord's help we will.

No one can answer the question of what God will speak to you, but we do know some of the things God will speak to you about. First, God will speak to you about where you are. God knows everything about you; out of the almost eight billion people on earth at this very moment, God knows where you are right now. Because He knows how to find you, he will often speak to you about where you currently are. Perhaps that means where you are spiritually. When you became a Christian, the conviction you felt was God speaking to you about where you were in sin. God will speak to where you are in ministry. Sometimes this means God calls you into ministry for the first time, or maybe He redirects your ministry. Often, God also will speak to you about things that you have been doing that are not pleasing to Him and how He wants you to change the direction of your life. God often will speak to His children about where they are in hopes to draw them closer to Himself.

The Lord will also often speak to you about where you are going. In the life of Abram, God spoke to him several times about his future. In fact, as we will talk about at length in upcoming chapters, God shared His own great plan for humanity through Abram. In order for this great plan to begin, as stated, it meant Abram would have to leave where he was and journey to an unknown place. While it was unknown to Abram, God knew what He was doing the whole time and where He was taking Abram. Just as the Lord spoke to Abram, so He will speak to you. God is a good Father who desires to tell us what we need to know so we can experience the greatest good and great blessing in our lives.

So how will God speak to you? Perhaps the Lord will speak in an audible voice as He has done to those in the past. Perhaps He will speak to you down deep in your Spirit where you just know and understand God is speaking like we previously described. Or maybe while reading your Bible God supernaturally speaks to you by highlighting what you are reading and applying it to your life. Maybe God gives you a dream, a vision, or perhaps God gives someone else a word of knowledge to come speak to you. In whatever way God chooses to speak to you, rest assured it will be for your good.

Chapter 2 - A Deeper Look

Have you ever had the Lord speak to you? What did He say and how did it impact your life?

_____

_____

_____

_____

_____

_____

When you begin to wonder what God might speak to you, what excites you the most?

_____

_____

_____

_____

_____

_____

_____

God Speaks to Abram

What are you praying about right now that you need God to speak to you about? Write it down and ask God every day to speak to you.

_____

_____

_____

_____

_____

Can you find places in the Bible where God spoke to people who were needing to hear from Him? How does that encourage you?

_____

_____

_____

_____

_____

_____

Chapter 3

God's Promise and Assurance

"Do not be afraid, Abram. I am your shield, your exceedingly great reward"
(Gen. 15:1, emphasis added).

Genesis fifteen records at least the third time that God has spoken to Abram that we know of. It could be that God poke to Abram more than three times, but by this point, Abram has some experiences with the voice of the Lord. He has had some interaction with the Lord and has heard the types of things God speaks of. The third recorded conversation God has with Abram in Genesis fifteen is not unlike the first two times God spoke to him, at least to begin with.

As we previously discussed, the first time we read of God speaking to Abram is in Genesis twelve. In this amazing conversation that God had with Abram, God told him to get out of his homeland, that God would bless him and make him a great nation, and that God would bless everyone who blessed him and curse whoever curses him (Gen 12:1-3). What an amazing first introduction with the voice of the Lord. How amazing to be given such a word from the Lord. I am sure that Abram felt unworthy, grateful, and extremely excited about what God was going to soon bring to pass. The words God spoke must have been so powerful and meaningful to Abram because the writer of Genesis, Moses, said as soon as God finished speaking to Abram that first time, "...Abram departed as the Lord had spoken" (Gen. 12:3).

That simple sentence blows my mind. How incredible that after less than eighty spoken words from the Lord Abram was not only convinced it was the Lord speaking to him, but the very first action of Abram was to obey. Abram's reaction is so encouraging to me. It makes me look at my own life and actions. It also makes me pray and ask the Lord to help me be a person who would not hesitate to obey His voice.

The second time God spoke to Abram is found in the next chapter, Genesis thirteen, after Abram unselfishly allowed Lot, his nephew, to have first pick of the land around Canaan. The Lord came to Abram and in this exchange, God tells Abram the land as far as he can see in every direction has been given to him and his descendants (Gen 13:14-17). Again, what an amazing word from the Lord! What a blessing from the Lord! Abram's flocks and household have grown to such a size that he needed a large piece of land for all that God already blessed him with. This is the reason why Abram's family and flocks had to separate from Lot and his family and flocks; there was not enough room for them both. Not only did God give Abram the land he needed, but the Lord blessed him with so much more. God told him that his descendants would be equal to the number of grains of sand on the earth and the number of stars in the sky. Again, what an amazing word from the Lord. God told Abram that his descendants would be more than he, or anyone else could number.

If the Lord came to you and told you what He told Abram, what would your reaction be? I am sure we would be excited and overjoyed at God's word. Would I accept and trust in such an astounding word from the Lord? Do I believe everything God says? To be transparent, I still have to pray and ask the Lord to help me in my unbelief, much like the man in Mark 9. It's not that I do not believe God can, it's that my mind often cannot comprehend how. I must admit, God is still working on me, and He still has a lot of work to do.

I love Abram's response once again. Moses records that Abram, after receiving the words from the Lord, "...built an altar there to the Lord" (Gen. 13:19). What a beautiful response. Abram worshiped. We are not told that Abram uttered a word to the Lord, but instead built an altar and worshiped. He gave thanks to God for being so kind, for being so loving and good. He honored the Lord by once again showing the Lord that

He was first in his life and that whatever the Lord desired for him, he accepted. Again, the Word brings conviction to my heart. God help me, help us all, to have faith like Abram.

The third time Moses records God speaking to Abram, as I said, is in Genesis fifteen. This time God speaks to Abram in a vision. I love that God comes to Abram differently than the first two times. It shows how God desires to speak to His people in all types of ways. Our heavenly Father is not limited; throughout Scripture, God chooses to speak to His people in all types of ways, and some of them are even comical. In Abram's life, God spoke to him this third time through a vision.

God also uses His Word to speak to His people. Paul said, "All Scripture *is* given by inspiration of God, and *is* profitable for doctrine, for reproof, for correction, for instruction in righteousness, that the man of God may be complete, thoroughly equipped for every good work" (1 Tim. 3:16-17, emphasis added). So many people today desire a "word" from God about their lives or situation, but those same people seldom open up God's Word and read what He says. The Bible is God's very breath penned on paper. It is the very "word" we are seeking from the Lord.

God has also chosen to speak to people in other ways. God spoke to David through the prophet Nathan. One of the most powerful moments in the Old Testament is when God used Nathan to speak to David and told him, "…you are the man" (2 Sam. 2:17). God also uses the Holy Spirit to speak to us down deep in our spirits. This voice that speaks to us individually is often not audible to others, yet the voice is clear and powerful in our hearts. God even opened the mouth of a donkey and spoke to Balaam in the book of Numbers (see 22:31-38).

There are a number of ways God can and will speak to His people. There is no doubt that God desires to speak to you because He loves you and wants to help you. This was the case in Abram's life as well. The third time God spoke to Abram was in a vision, when God first spoke words of blessing and comfort to him.

Do Not Be Afraid

God first tells Abram, "Do not be afraid" (Gen. 15:1). Multiple times in Scripture when a supernatural visitation occurs, the first words from the Lord or angel are, "Do not afraid," or, "Fear not." It shows that God indeed knows us. He knows that often our first reaction to something or someone we do not comprehend is fear. We fear what we do not understand, and God knows our thoughts and emotions, so the first Divine words often uttered are, "Do not fear."

The Lord's statement to Abram is not just a greeting, but also a command. God spoke emphatically to Abram in saying, "Do not be afraid." In other words, do not allow yourself to become fearful. The enemy would have loved nothing more than for Abram to be so overcome with fear in that moment that he ran away from the Lord's presence and thus His voice.

Satan would love nothing more than for you to do the same. Satan often tries to paint a picture of God as being a great big beast with uncontrollable fury. He tries to make us afraid of interacting with God, speaking with God, and listening for His voice. The enemy of our souls does this because he knows God desires to bless and guide His people. Satan desires your life to unravel and God desires for your life to have direction.

God speaks to Abram and commands him to not be afraid. Fear does not come from God as Paul reminded Timothy, "For God has not given us a spirit of fear..." (2 Tim. 2:17). If we are overcome with fear, it will cause us to be ineffective in our walk with God. Fear freezes its victims and leaves them incapacitated. God's desire for His people is to be free from fear so we may hear what He has to say and begin to walk in His direction.

Perhaps you are reading this book and you are dealing with an overwhelming sense of fear. Maybe you are fearful of what God has asked you to do. Perhaps you are fearful of the future and what will happen if you obey God's voice. Or perhaps you are fearful because of what you see occurring all around you. Beloved, God's word to you is the same as His word to Abram, "Do not be afraid!"

I know what you're thinking. You are thinking, "Easy for you to say, you don't know what I am going through." That is very true; I do not know what you are dealing with at this moment, nor do I know what God has asked of you. However, I want you to think for a moment, what has been the character of God that you have seen? When you read Scripture, or when you hear the testimonies of others, what have you heard of the Lord and His actions? Have you ever heard that God caused some terrible calamity to occur to people who loved Him? Have you ever read in Scripture where God ignored the prayers of His people? Has God ever wished or intended for evil to fall upon people who called on His name? NEVER! God loves His people. God loves YOU! And because He loves you, He desires the best for you.

Being fearful is not sinful. Again, it is often our first reaction, and it is often something we cannot help. Our fallen nature and imperfect emotions often default to fear, however, fear can lead us to disobedience, which is sinful.[6] You and I cannot afford to allow fear to take hold of our lives and forever paralyze us spiritually, when God has so much for us to do and so many blessings in store for us. God has proven throughout Scripture that He is trustworthy. We can depend on Him to lead us in the right direction. If you take a few moments to stop and think about what God has done

---

[6] David Roper, *Seeing God: Meet God In the Unexpected* (Grand Rapids, MI, Discovery House Publishers, 2006) 102.

in your life, I am confident you will remember that God has proved Himself trustworthy to you, as well.

In fact, let me ask you to do a quick exercise. Get a piece of paper or open a new note in your phone or tablet. Write down all the times God has answered a prayer, worked out a situation, blessed you even when you did not ask for a blessing, and any other great thing that has occurred in your life. I promise you it will encourage you. You will remember that God has blessed you and come through for you time after time. When we remember the character of God, fear simply cannot stay.

Do you remember King Jehoshaphat and how the Lord delivered the Children of Israel in 2 Chronicles chapter twenty? King Jehoshaphat gets word that three armies have joined forces, and they are on their way to Israel to destroy Jerusalem and to kill him. Jehoshaphat was a human being just like you and me, and when he was informed of the enemy's advances against him and his people, he had the same reaction that you and I have so often: Fear gripped his heart.

The King displays the reaction that you and I should have today when we are overwhelmed with fear. Jehoshaphat runs to the Lord. "And Jehoshaphat feared, and set himself to seek the Lord, and proclaimed a fast throughout all Judah" (2 Chronicles 20:3). The King stands up on the steps of the temple with a great crowd gathered in the courtyard and he beings to cry out to the Lord. He prays an incredible prayer, and he was so honest with the Lord about how he felt. Read what he prays:

"O Lord God of our fathers, are You not God in heaven, and do You not rule over all the kingdoms of the nations, and in Your hand is there not power and might, so that no one is able to withstand You? Are You not our God, who drove out the inhabitants of this land before Your people Israel, and gave it to the descendants of Abraham Your friend forever? And they dwell in it and have built You a sanctuary in it for Your name, saying, 'If disaster comes upon us—sword, judgment, pestilence, or famine—we will stand before this temple and in Your presence (for Your name is in this temple), and cry out to You in our affliction, and You will hear and save.' And now, here are the people of Ammon, Moab, and Mount Seir—whom You would not let Israel invade when they came out of the land of Egypt, but they turned from them and did not destroy them— here they are, rewarding us by coming to throw us out of Your possession which You have given us to inherit. O our God, will You not judge them? For we have no power against this great multitude that is coming against us; nor do we know what to do, but our eyes are upon You" (2 Chro. 3:6-12)

Jehoshaphat was saying, God I am scared, I don't know how we are going to make it out of this, I don't understand what you are doing in this case, but God I STILL TRUST YOU!

He prayed, my eyes are on you, you are our only hope, if you don't do it, we are going to perish, so God I trust you. When Jehoshaphat finished praying, the next verse says that the king and all the people stood before the Lord. The Bible gives the indication that they were all standing in reverence, waiting in anticipation for the Lord to answer.

The Spirit of the Lord moves upon Jahaziel and begins to speak about this mighty work that God was about to do. The Lord speaks and says, "You will not need to fight in this battle. Position yourselves, stand still and see the salvation of the Lord, who is with you, O Judah and Jerusalem!' Do not fear or be dismayed; tomorrow go out against them, for the Lord is with you" (2 Chro. 3 17-18). The Lord told the people of Israel to trust Him, and watch what He can do. The next day, the three armies assemble to march against Israel, but Scripture says that the Lord sent ambushes against the enemy, and they turned on each other and utterly destroyed each other. The Lord proved once again that His people did not have to fear because He would take care of all of them—and all of us.

God told Abram, "Do not be afraid," because, as I said, God knew Abram's default emotion was fear, so God addressed that from the very start of His address to him. The Psalmist said, "God *is* our refuge and strength, A very present help in trouble. Therefore, we will not fear even though the earth be removed, And though the mountains be carried into the midst of the sea; *Though* its waters roar *and* be troubled, *Though* the mountains shake with its swelling" (Ps. 46:1-3, emphasis added). Why does the Psalmist say that we "will not fear"? Because it is God we are depending on. If we had to depend on our own strength, then we would have so much to fear, but we have God, the Creator of the universe, on our side, therefore we WILL NOT fear!

I am Your Shield

After the Lord speaks to Abram and tells him to not be afraid, God continues His discourse by saying, "I am your shield" (Gen. 15:1). This occurrence from the Lord no doubt brought great comfort to the life of Abram as he continued to follow the voice of the Lord. This self-description the Lord spoke to Abram gives us a picture of God encircling Himself around Abram, as a shield, to protect him and his household from attacks of enemies. One of the most encouraging parts of this story is that Abram has not asked the Lord to protect him. God decided to be a shield or protector on His own because He cared for Abram.

A year ago, my family and I were traveling home from a speaking engagement, and we were on an interstate in north Georgia. Traveling on the interstate, my speed was somewhere around seventy to seventy-five miles per hour, and I was traveling in the far left-hand lane. To my right on the side of the road I noticed a deer come from out of the woods and begin walking on the six-lane interstate. I saw the deer far enough in advance to begin slowing down as the deer continued to walk across the lanes from my right to my left. Seeing what the deer was doing, I started to get over in the right lanes hoping to pass by it. Unfortunately, as deer so often do, when I approached it, the deer turned back as if it was going back to the woods and I clipped the deer with the driver's side fender. Unfortunately, the deer succumbed to injury and a highway service came to render the road safe. Thankfully, not only was my family ok, but the damage to my car was very minimal and we were able to make it home safely.

I have thought about that incident many times since, and I thank the Lord for keeping us protected. Driving home that day, I wish I could say my family and I were singing along to worship songs, or we were in prayer driving down the road, but to be honest, we were just trying to get home. I don't recall exactly what our minds were on, but with three kids under the age of six in the car, I'm sure someone was crying, or laughing, or playing. If you are a parent, you understand exactly what I am talking about. My point is, even when my mind was perhaps far from worship, prayer, or God's word, my Shield was still very present.

When the Lord told Abram in Genesis fifteen that He is his shield, it was a promise that as long as Abram was in relationship with Him, God would always be his protector. It was not a promise that nothing bad would happen; Abram was a human living in a fallen world. In the hardest of times, God would see Abram through, and indeed He did all the days of his life.

Abram had already experienced the kind of protection the Lord provided when Abram waged the first recorded war in the Bible. In the chapter prior, Genesis 14, Abram's nephew Lot was taken captive and when Abram learned of the situation he took 318 of his own men from his household and pursued the armies that had taken Lot captive. The Bible says that Abram and "his servants attacked them and pursued them as far as Hobah which is north of Damascus. So he brought back all the goods and also brought back his bother Lot and his goods, as well as the women and the people" (Gen. 14:15-16).

In your life and mine, God is still the same. Being in relationship with the Lord means He is our protector. No one can convince me God was not present when that deer decided to cross the interstate in front of my family and me in our car. I believe with all my heart that God was my protector that day. I also believe that if you look back over your life, you will see the Shield that has protected you over and over.

I am Your Exceedingly Great Reward

God ends His opening remarks to Abram in Genesis 15:1 by declaring that He is not only his protector, but also his exceedingly great reward. What an incredible word from the Lord! Up to this point, God has already blessed Abram so much with wealth, herds and flocks of all types of animals, servants, land

and much more. When Abram left Egypt after lying to Pharaoh, and God brought great plagues upon Pharaoh's household, which we will later discuss in detail, Abram left Egypt with great wealth. The Bible says, "So Pharaoh commanded his men concerning him; and they sent him away with his wife and all he had (Gen 12:20). The Bible goes on to say Abram was very rich in livestock, in silver, and in gold" (Gen. 13:2). It is after all these events that God tells Abram, "I am your exceedingly great reward." (Gen 15:1). God was telling Abram that although he did not fully understand what God was saying in that moment, He had so much more with which to bless him. God's blessings, of course, began with blessing Abram with a son, but the rewards God had for Abram did not start and end with a baby boy. God would soon overwhelm Abram's life with blessings.

God's desire to bless His people is intrinsic, unquestionable. There is nothing you have to do that will make God desire to bless you. There are things, like obeying His commands, that will bring more blessings into your life, but nothing could make Him desire to bless you anymore than He already does.

I travel a great deal and my children know when I go on some trips they most likely will receive a small toy or candy upon my return. My wife has often told me that I spoil the kids, but to be honest I cannot help it. I love them so much. I love making them happy. I love the smiles on their faces when I reach in my bag and pull out some goodie. My children are the light of my life. They bring joy to my heart on the hardest and most stressful of days. I love giving them gifts.

Our Heavenly Father is much the same. He desires to bless you and me because He is good. David said at the close of his most famous Psalm, "Surely goodness and mercy shall follow me all the days of my life" (Ps. 23:6). Why could David be so confident in the blessings of goodness and mercy following him throughout his life? It is because God is good and there is no other way God can be. Scripture further declares, "Oh, give thanks to the Lord, for *He is* good! For His mercy *endures* forever" (1 Chron. 16:34, emphasis added). Wherever you are today and in whatever condition, praise Him for being good.

Take time to pray and share your appreciation to the Lord for blessing you. Are you saved? Thank Him! Are you alive? Thank Him! Have you eaten today? Thank Him! Do you have money in your bank account? Thank Him! Give the Lord praise for being your exceedingly great reward.

God would soon bring the promised son, Isaac, into the world of Abram, and this tremendous blessing would only be the beginning of the great reward God would bring into his life. When Abram's life was over on this side of Heaven, he entered into his eternal reward. Beloved, if you know Jesus as your personal Savior, then you too have an exceedingly great reward awaiting you. Jesus said, "Let not your heart be troubled; you believe in God, believe also in Me. In My

Father's house are many mansions; if *it were* not *so,* I would have told you. I go to prepare a place for you. And if I go and prepare a place for you…" (Jn. 14:1-3, emphasis added). One day you and I are going to go to our heavenly home that Christ has prepared for us. To God be the glory for what He has in store for us.

A Moment of Wonder

How incredible is it that the King of the universe desires nothing more than to speak to us? God has never intended for us to live our lives without His guidance and blessing. For Abram, God came to him, called him out of his hometown, and challenged him to follow His voice. As I said, the first thing God said to Abram was to not be afraid. Remember, the enemy wants to paralyze you with fear, but God desires to free you from fear. For Abram, it must have been so assuring that when God speaks, he had nothing to be afraid of. This is a lesson that Abram had to be reminded of over and over. You and I are no different. Again today, we need to know that when God speaks He always has our best interest in mind, so we need not be afraid of God speaking to us. For my family, 2023 was the year we began to hear the voice of the Lord speaking, and it shocked us all.

While I was in the middle of writing this book, my family and I were contemplating making one of the biggest moves of our lives. At the beginning of 2023, my wife and I began sensing the Lord preparing us for a change. It is hard to fully describe what we felt, but it was a feeling of how things might—and very likely were—going to change. We began having discussions that started with, "What if God did _____." Our minds just began to fill in the blank with all kinds of things. What if God moved us away from the denomination we have always served in? What if God moved us to a new city or town? We would think of all kinds of things and allow our minds to dream.

In the Fall of 2023, I received a phone call from a church consulting company who was trying to help two churches find someone for positions. One of the positions was as a finance pastor and the other was as a discipleship pastor. Both positions were at mega-churches that are very well respected. The arrival of the opportunities was flattering but not shocking, as again the Lord had started communicating with me and my wife that things were going to change. We prayed about the two opportunities but we never received confirmation from the Lord that those were our next step. A third opportunity came in the early spring of 2024. A church contacted me about coming on board with their staff to oversee the launch of their new college. I immediately was intrigued by this opportunity and my wife and I began to pray for the Lord to guide us once again to know His will.

One Sunday at church, our pastor preached a message about peace and how God will fill our lives with peace as we live for Him. In one particular part of the sermon, our pastor shared about how we should allow "peace to be our guide" when we are seeking answers and direction for our lives. That message has prevailed to us so much while we have been trying to hear the voice of the Lord about all the opportunities we have seen. When the position of leading a college was presented to us, not only did we have a great sense of exhilaration, but as we began to pray, our hearts were filled with peace. It has been a peace that has guided us to know this opportunity is from the Lord and it is His will for our lives. The peace we received was assurance that God is with us and it also was a promise of God's abiding presence will be with us in the days, weeks, months, and years ahead. While we are still living out this great adventure, I am so grateful for God's promises and assurance.

Chapter 3 - A Deeper Look

What promises or word has the Lord spoken to you?

_____

_____

_____

_____

_____

_____

Have you had to fight off fear? What helped you overcome it?

_____

_____

_____

_____

_____

_____

Remind yourself of a time the Lord was a shield in your life. What did God do to bring protection in your life or your family's lives?

_____

_____

_____

_____

_____

_____

_____

When has the Lord done something unexpected in your life and changed the direction of your life?

_____

_____

_____

_____

_____

_____

_____

Chapter 4

Honest Abram

But Abram said, "Lord God, what will you give me, seeing I go childless, and the heir of my house is Eliezer of Damascus?"
(Genesis 15:2, emphasis added).

In the Summer of 2016, my wife, Anna Kate, and I were getting ready for thirty young adults to arrive at our house and we were running a little behind, which was not a surprise. At the church I pastored we were in the middle of our community group gatherings where our small group came together to hang out, eat, laugh, and have fun for a few hours. It was a season of growth for us at the church. God was doing wonderful things and while our numbers were increasing, greater still was the spiritual growth we were experiencing. On this particular day, the young adults were coming to our house and we were rushing to complete all the last minute details, clean up, finish the food, and finally get our baths and prepare for everyone to arrive. I was getting ready and I heard Anna Kate gasp. I yelled,

"What is it?" She brought me a pregnancy test that had a positive faint pink line. Anna Kate was pregnant with our first child.

We were ecstatic and overwhelmed with joy! It was a wonderful moment that still brings tears to my eyes when I recall it. Our story is like so many others in America today. For six years prior to receiving the amazing news that our first child was on the way, Anna Kate and I rode an emotional roller coaster about having a child. What I remember most about those years is my heart breaking for Anna Kate as each month brought a wave of hope that said, "Maybe this month." When I began writing this portion of this book, I wanted Anna Kate to share part of her testimony and I am so proud to have her write and encourage you.

Anna Kate's Testimony

At age 17, I received a health diagnosis I feared would affect my dreams of a family. However, I brushed off the worries because of my age, and I naively thought it would not happen to me. Matt and I both always agreed we wanted several children, and we wanted to start our family soon. Soon took a lot longer than we expected. During those years of waiting, there were innumerable prayers sent up by us and others. I cannot count the times we went up for special prayer or the times we spent praying alone. I could not understand amid the pain what was wrong. Honestly, I became angry.

I constantly had dialogue with God. Many questions came out, but I could not receive the answers. As a pastor's wife, I dedicated my life to the ministry. I did everything in my power to serve the Lord as best I could. My greatest and most persistent question to God became, "How can you not answer our prayer when we do so much for You?" Writing it down makes it sound so brash, but after years of waiting on an answer to prayer I was frustrated. God was patient. He showed me grace, listened to my questions, and sent me encouragement.

A few months into 2016, I began reading a book about prayer. I prayed and tried my best to trust God. Our hearts were aching together because we were nearing what we felt like would be the last time I would take medication for a while. The monthly roller coaster was too much, and we needed a break. I still did not have an answer to my questions, and I felt as though God was silent. I continued being faithful to His work and put my trust in Him. The last month of medication worked. In June 2016, we found out we were expecting. February 27, 2017, Elia Kate was born. Our prayers were answered.

Reflecting on those years and the heartache, I realized what I had forgotten. I was expecting an exchange. Do good work for the Lord, then He will answer my prayers. I wasn't working for Him just because He was my Savior, I was expecting benefits. I forgot about His omniscience. I forgot to be thankful for His mercy and grace providing me salvation. I forgot that salvation is enough, and if another one of my prayers was never answered it would still be enough. I forgot that I am undeserving, but He makes me worthy. I now remember, every day looking at a blue-eyed-curly-haired little girl, that He is merciful despite my faults, and He still answers prayers.

The Lord has now blessed Anna Kate and me with three beautiful children. They are a testimony of the power of prayer and the goodness of God. Elia Kate, Edyth Ray, and Ephraim Franklin are daily reminders to me to thank the Lord for all He has done and to remember that there is no situation too hard for God. I am so grateful for the gifts that God has blessed us with. The Bible declares "Behold, children *are* a heritage from the LORD, The fruit of the womb *is* a reward" (Ps. 127:3, emphasis added). I have found this to be true and I am so thankful for God's amazing goodness.

I am so grateful that when Anna and I were honest with the Lord, He did not dismiss our concerns. I am grateful that our Heavenly Father did not look at us as being disrespectful. God knew our hearts and how we loved Him. I am thankful that in our relationship with God we can be open and honest with Him. When Abram opened up and responded to the Lord, it was not exactly what you and I might have expected.

Abram Speaks to the Lord

In the previous two times the Lord had spoken to Abram, there was no reply. Abram simply received the word from the Lord and obeyed. When the Lord speaks to Abram for the third time in Genesis fifteen, Abram responds to the Lord for the first time and his response is somewhat shocking.

The Lord shares with Abram how He desires to bless him, saying, "I am your shield, your exceedingly great reward" (Gen. 15:1). Then Scripture shares Abram's response: "But Abram said, 'Lord God, what will you give me, seeing I go childless, and the heir of my house is Eliezer of Damascus?'" (Gen. 15:2). But Abram's frustration does not stop there; he continues, "Look, you have given me no offspring; indeed one born in my house is my heir!" (Gen 15:3). There is not a great deal known about Eliezer other than he was a servant in Abram's house and most likely born of parents who were servants to Abram. Because Abram and Sarai had no natural child, Abram had concluded, should he and Sarai pass away, all of their positions would have to go to Eliezer. In fact, it was a custom of that day that the head of a house could name the person who would inherit the estate if no natural heir was available.[7]

You can hear the frustration in Abram's voice as he responds to the Lord's greeting. I know you can understand what Abram is saying. You may not have walked in Abram's shoes, but you too have been overwhelmed. At some point, I know you also know what it is like to think your life is going to go in one direction, but a phone call, diagnosis, or problem arises and completely changes everything. Before we condemn or think badly of Abram's reaction, may we also remember what it is like to be in such a moment as he was. Abram opens his heart to the Lord to reveal exactly how he was feeling and what was on his mind. Here is one of the most beautiful things about being in

---

[7] Henry Halley. Halley's Bible Handbook. (Grand Rapids: Zondervan, 1965)

a relationship with someone who deeply cares and loves you. You can be honest with them.

I want to encourage you today that you can be open and honest with the Lord. You do not have to put up a front with the Lord and try to make it seem like everything is ok when your heart is breaking. You do not have to walk on eggshells with the Lord and be afraid that God cannot handle your honesty or be concerned to upset Him by being honest. No, you can bare your heart to Him and know that He will not respond like a kid with a magnifying glass trying to zap some ants. No, beloved, He loves you and He already knows what is on your mind.

Be Honest With God Because He is Omniscient

Have you ever been speaking to someone and they finish your sentence for you? It has happened to me a few times and my response was, "Yes! Exactly!" When you talk to someone who has been through what you are going through or knows what it is like to be in your shoes, there is a sense of relief that comes when you talk to them. I want to encourage you that you can be honest with the Lord because He knows what is going on in your life already. There is nothing that the Lord is not aware of. God does not turn on the news channel each day to catch up on current events, see who is leading in the polls, or learn what the weather is doing. God knows all! We have a word that describes this attribute of the Lord: omniscient. God is omniscient, all-knowing. David addressed this attribute of the Lord in Psalm 139, "O Lord, You have searched me and known *me*. You know my sitting down and my rising up; You understand my thought afar off" (Ps. 139:1-2, emphasis added). I love how David begins his thoughts by saying that God has searched him and has come to know him. Beloved, God is no different with you.

Some of you might say, "I'm not the King of Israel. God doesn't pay attention to me like He did David." While you are not the King of Israel you are certainly as important to the Lord. We know from God's own Word that He is no respecter of persons (Acts 10:34). The attention, time, and care that He gave to David, He also gives to you. David said God "has searched me and knows me."

God knows you. YES, you! He knows your personality, your attributes, your weaknesses, the number of hairs on your head, and every single detail of your life. In the time we are living in, many would protest God knowing the intimate details of our lives and call it intrusive, but God does not know us for the sake of being intrusive; He knows us because He desires to help us!

You can be open and honest with the Lord because He knows you! He knows the situation you are facing and all the factors involved. David said it best, "You comprehend my path and my lying down, And are acquainted with all my ways" (Ps. 139:3). God is acquainted, He knows all of your ways. Because He knows all, why would we try to act like everything is ok when we pray, but we are burdened or lonely? God knows already. Why try to sweep things under a rug? God sees the mess under the rug. GOD KNOWS ALL!

This fact should not bring any type of condemnation or anxiety. We should rejoice that God knows everything. Even in my failures and sin, I am grateful that God knows all. So when I go to Him in repentance, He already knows all about the situation that led up to my sin. He can instruct and mold me to become stronger in the area where I was weak. Beloved, rejoice that God knows all about you.

Be Honest with God Because He is Omnipotent

I currently work and serve the church by leading the Mission USA office for the Congregational Holiness Church. The Mission USA oversees all CH churches within the United States as well as a host of other things. Each April, the department reaches out to churches and individuals during our annual fundraiser event. There are some people and companies whom God has blessed financially and who have a gift of giving. I always reach out to those I know who are like this and share the specific needs and opportunities the department has and how they can contribute to the work of the Lord. I do this because I know they have the ability (power) to significantly impact our fundraising efforts. One gift from them could and does change our whole fundraiser. In similar ways, one touch from the Lord, one word from His throne, can change everything in your life.

Until Genesis fifteen, Abram has not spoken a reply to the Lord, or at least one is not recorded. When he responds to the Lord, Abram is honest with the Lord and tells Him the things that concern him the most. Abram was comfortable with opening up to the Lord because he had experienced the mighty power of the Lord in the past.

Abram was the great-to-the-eighth-grandson of Noah. There is no doubt that the Flood and all that God did on the earth in Noah's day were taught to Abram and to those in the cities and communities Abram traveled. If the great stories of Noah and the Flood were not enough to tell Abram of God's great power, there were the situations that God worked in Abram's favor to think about. We have previously discussed the wild moments in Abram's journey as he went down to Egypt. Out of fear, Abram concocted the idea to lie and tell everyone, including Pharaoh, that Sarai was his sister rather than sharing the truth of her being his wife. Even when Abram made a very unwise decision, God was with him and Sarai. When the truth of the situation came to light, Abram was allowed to keep all of the livestock, wealth, and goods Pharaoh gave him in exchange for his "sister". God blessed Abram abundantly in spite of his bad decisions.

Do you know what it is like to be blessed in spite of your bad decisions? I know I do! God has been so good to me and has blessed me and my family even though there have been countless bad decisions. Abram left Egypt more abundantly blessed than when he arrived. Not only was Abram blessed when he left Egypt, but also while he was there God supernaturally worked out a situation that was almost disastrous.

Before Abram and Sarai arrived in Egypt, Abram explained to Sarai what he wanted to do. He told her they were going to tell everyone that she was his sister. However, this did not prevent Sarai being taken to be intended for Pharaoh. Sarai was taken and when this occurred, God intervened. One of the most amazing facts about this story is that it is not recorded that Abram ever went before the Lord and asked the Lord to intervene. It is not that Abram did not desire God to work this situation out; Abram was distraught. Can you imagine this happening to you and your spouse? To have his spouse taken by the most powerful man in the most powerful kingdom in the world must have been beyond scary. Have you ever been so worried or scared you did not know what to pray or how to pray for the situation? I think this could be where Abram was in Genesis twelve. I am not sure I would be able to think, talk, or act. I would be so broken and scared. However, even though it is not recorded that Abram cried out to the Lord, God moved and His power brought the mightiest man in the world to his knees.

I am not sure what situation you may be facing as you are reading these words, but I want to encourage you that the same God who moved in Abram's life can also move for you today. It absolutely does not matter how dire your situation may look today, nothing and no one can stand in the presence of your Heavenly Father. When He speaks, mountains melt, stars appear, and even Satan himself has to bow his knee. God is more than able to bring a solution to the problem you are facing.

In Genesis fifteen, Abram once again is burdened and worried. He opens his heart to the Lord and lays it all out on the table. There were no secrets and Abram did not allow anything to be hidden from the Lord. I believe it is because Abram knew that the God he was speaking to had the ability and power to change his circumstances. No doubt Abram had to wonder, *God, you have waited so long, I'm old, Sarai's old.* His next thought had to be, *but I have seen You move before; I cannot deny Your power.*

How have you seen God move in your life? What has He done for you before? Has He not amazed you? Has He not shown that no circumstances can stop Him? No beloved, nothing can stop our God. You can be honest with Him because He is all-powerful, omnipotent. There is nothing He cannot do. So open your heart. Lay it all on the table today. He already knows what you are feeling and what you are thinking and He can do something about it all.

Be Honest with God Because it Brings Relief

I recently went to lunch with a pastor who had been going through a hard time with a few church members.

Honest Abram

I knew some of the context prior to our meeting, and as we sat down I asked him to share with me what he could. I am grateful that he trusted me enough to open up. After sharing the situation, I was able to share with him my thoughts and relay some situations I had been through that were similar to his. When our lunch was over, I asked him how he felt, and he said something that has stuck with me. He said, "Oh, man, I feel so much better. I just needed to talk to someone who would understand."

I have thought about that statement a great deal, because I knew exactly what he meant. I have felt like that many times after I spoke to someone I could trust; it did bring a sense of relief after I talked through what was bothering me the most. It helps to talk.

May I add caution to your thoughts? There are many people around you with whom you cannot be honest. In fact, it would be to your advantage if you were not open and honest with many around you. Unfortunately, there are those who would love nothing more than to try and hurt you with what you tell them. There are those who would love to take advantage of your situation by sharing on social media what you said or what you are going through. We must be careful whom we open up to and what we share with that person. There is someone in your life, however, to whom you can open up and share what is taking place in your life. I encourage you to find someone you not only can talk to, but who will also pray for you.

Last, let me encourage you to be a person someone can come to. As we just discussed, you need someone you can talk to, so you be the person for someone else. This perhaps means that you pray and ask the Lord to help you with telling everyone what you know. No one will trust you if they know you are going to tell everything you have heard to the first person you run into. Ask the Lord for strength and then listen to the "still small voice" in your spirit that will nudge you and tell you, "Don't say that." Have courage to listen to His voice. Discipline yourself to obey the Lord. Just as you need a trustworthy friend, so do others. Be an encouraging friend to someone and pray for those who confide in you.

A Moment of Wonder

In 2014, my wife came to me and said she felt she was supposed to quit her job and be a homemaker. My wife is incredibly skilled in making things. She can make some of the most beautiful things with almost any medium. I have seen her create a beautiful panting, build shelfs with scrap wood and power tools, bake, and decorate stunning cookies for parties, and much more. God has given her a gift and she uses it to bring glory to the Lord. However, when she came to me and told me she really felt the Lord wanted her to quit her job, I thought she had lost her mind! At the start, I thought, *she cannot really be serious. God had blessed her with a great job with a great deal of promise for promotion and advancement.* I remember thinking, *millionaires quit their jobs, not young families just getting started in life.* We had only become husband and wife just four years prior. We had only begun to build our lives together. I was pastoring a small church in Alabama at the time, and I still worked for my father's pest control business. While the Lord had blessed us greatly financially, I could not see how the numbers worked.

One of the major reasons I was so hesitant was that we had plans to take a trip to Israel that same year, and while many blessed us with a gift to help us go, we obviously were trying to save thousands of dollars to finish paying for this trip. I remember telling Anna, "This idea is crazy, we will have to cancel our Israel trip." Weeks went by; the subject would come up from time to time, and it would cause some tense moments in our home. I remember going to a church service at our local campground and going to the altar and pouring out my heart to God. I was tired of worrying about money, I was tired of worrying about upsetting Anna Kate. I had to know that night what to do. Before the minister gave the altar call, I ran down to the front of the church and fell at the altar. I opened my heart to the Lord and was as open and honest as I could be. I told the Lord how worried and scared I was about how we would pay our bills. I cried out to Him, sharing how I did not understand why He would be leading my wife to quit her job. I cried so many tears my eyes began to swell. I was broken and open before the Lord. While I was praying, there was a peace that filled my heart. I cannot adequately explain it to you, but somehow I knew everything was going to be ok. When I got up from the altar there were three different individuals who come up to me that night and spoke words of encouragement to me. One said, "Matthew, God wants you to trust Him and not the numbers." Another said, "Matthew, if you are worried about finances remember that God shall supply all your need according to His riches in glory by Christ Jesus" (Phil. 4:19). The last person said, "Matthew, I feel the Lord wants me to remind you that everything will be ok. Trust the Lord, and He will take care of you and your family." I am not sure what your theology might be on a story like this, but for me, those were words from the Lord, sent for me at a moment when I had no clue what to do.

I went home from church and told my wife she could turn her notice in and quit her job. Within a few days, we had countless people, some we did not know well, give us fistfuls of money. People would come to our home and write checks for hundreds of dollars. We would receive checks in the mail and even in town a few times. It was amazing, and a little wild to be honest. God absolutely proved to me that He is my sustainer. He is the one who will keep and provide for my family.

Let me encourage you, open to the Lord. If you do not know Christ as your Savior, then your first step is to ask Christ to forgive you. You will never find a more loving Father than our Heavenly Father. Share you heart with Him. Perhaps you are reading this and you know Christ as Savior, but you have not talked to Him in a while. Let me encourage you, talk to God. Pray and seek the Lord. You will find great relief and peace.

Chapter 4 - A Deeper Look

What is something that you need to be honest about that you have not talked about?

_____

_____

_____

_____

_____

_____

Have you ever had the Lord do something for you that blew your mind? Write it down and thank the Lord for His abilities.

_____

_____

_____

_____

_____

_____

What are three things you need God to do in your life today?

1.

_____

_____

_____

_____

_____

_____

2.

_____

_____

_____

_____

_____

_____

_____

3.

_____

_____

_____

_____

_____

_____

_____

How can you become a person that others can talk to and be honest with?

_____

_____

_____

_____

_____

_____

_____

_____

_____

Chapter 5

God's Response to Abram

And behold, the word of the Lord came to him, saying, "This one shall not be your heir, but one who will come from your own body shall be you heir."

(Genesis 15:4, emphasis added).

I wonder what was going through the mind of Moses as he wrote down the account of Abram encountering the voice of the Lord for the third time. Was he surprised by God's persistence? Did Abram's response to the Lord shock him? I suppose those are questions only eternity can answer, but the words of Moses seem to give us some insight into what he was thinking. The first eleven words of Genesis 15:4 are not the words of Abram, nor the Lord. These are the words of Moses, the words of commentary that Moses penned under the leading of the Spirit of God. Moses said, "...and behold, the word of the Lord came to him saying..." (Gen. 15:4). This verse, more precisely the first eleven words, is a transition in the conversation between God and Abram. The Lord has greeted Abram with a wonderful word. Abram responds, sharing how burdened he is because he has no son. God then shows us in His response several wonderful attributes that I am sure encouraged Abram and should also encourage us today.

I remember as a kid in about seventh grade struggling with grades in my English and reading classes. I loved school, mostly. If you asked me on a Monday morning, I probably would say I hated going to school, but truthfully I loved being around friends and playing sports. There were some concepts of certain subjects that I struggled to grasp. English was the worst. Understanding sentence agreements, breaking down complex sentences, and conjugation would easily make me drift off in some epic daydream. As a result, I remember getting my first "C" on my report card. What a gut-wrenching day for a seventh grader whose parents expected As with maybe the occasional B. I was terrified to show my parents. In those days, students would receive an actual piece of paper with the listing of classes and corresponding grades. Nothing was electronic and students had to have a parent or guardian sign the paper showing they at least saw the report. Students also had a week to have a parent sign the paper and return it to administrators. When I received my report card and I saw the C I received for my English class, I was petrified to show my parents. I was afraid of their response. Would they ground me? Would I get a whooping? I knew they would be disappointed in me, which was the worst part of all. I stretched that week out as long as possible and waited until the last day to show my mother my grades and have her sign the report. I pulled it out of my backpack and said, "Mom, here is my report card." I was expecting the worst, but my mother looked at me and calmly asked why I thought I made the grade I did in my English class. I shared with her I was having trouble. Then my mother told me something I have never forgotten. She told me, "I am proud of you, and I know you can work hard and bring your grade up. I believe in you and I am going to help you."

Wow! I had spent the last seven days in fear of the response I was going to get. I thought I would get a tongue lashing, an actually lashing, be grounded a few weeks, or some other punishment. When I was honest with my mother, she responded with a great deal of understanding and love. Have you ever had an experience similar to that? Perhaps it was in childhood or maybe it's been with your spouse or a friend. When a situation that you were sure was going to cause the person to be very upset and disappointed with you ends up with that person understanding and showing grace, it brings a great deal of relief.

In Genesis 15:4, I am not sure if Abram was nervous about how God would respond to his honesty, but Moses points out that the reader should not miss God's response. Moses uses the Hebrew word *hinneh* which is translated "behold."[8] Look at this, Moses decrees, pay attention to what is about to happen, to what God says and His reaction. Moses calls the reader to pull up close to see how God was resolute in His promises, despite the circumstances Abram presents before the Lord.

God Is Resolute Despite Circumstances

Moses wanted to encourage his readers to understand that God desired to continue the conversation He began with Abram. This tells us a little more about the amazing God we serve.

Think about the circumstances for Abram for a moment. Abram was seventy-five years old when God first spoke to him about his seed that was soon to come. Some contend that almost ten years had passed between Genesis twelve and Genesis fifteen. Abram was now eighty-five years old, and still waiting on the promise to come. By this point, Abram was discouraged and frustrated. His response pointed this out clearly. He opened his heart to the Lord and laid all his frustration on the table. The Lord responded, not in anger, but the Lord assured him that Abram's fear of living his whole life childless was without truth.

Be encouraged today that there is nothing that can happen in your life that takes the Lord by surprise; He always has and always will know what is best in your life. The Lord says, "Declaring the end from the

---

[8] https://biblehub.com/hebrew/2009.htm

beginning, And from ancient times things that are not yet done, Saying, 'My counsel shall stand, And I will do all My pleasure'" (Isaiah 46:10). The very fact God knows my end from the beginning also tells me that He knows all the circumstances surrounding every day of my life. He has an advantage over the enemy in our lives. While we can only see the problem from our point of view, the Lord sees the problem from His perspective. From God's perspective, it's not a matter of if, but when. God told Abram over and over the promised seed was coming. Abram already had a son (Ishmael); God was determining the right time for Isaac to be born.

From God's perspective the enemy had already lost. It is evident the enemy had worked on Abram's mind trying to convince him that God would never come through on His promise, but God's word is absolute. What He says will happen, will happen; Satan cannot prevent anything God says or does.

From God's perspective, He holds all of us in His arms. If we could discern the Spirit, we would be encouraged how the very arms of God are wrapped around us at all times. "The eternal God is thy refuge, and underneath are the everlasting arms" (Deuteronomy 33:27). Abram had experienced the protective arms of God multiple times by their encounter in Genesis fifteen. Were it not for the Lord, Abram and you and I would surely have been consumed by the plans of the enemy.

God's Response to Abram

The Lord is not fazed by any of the circumstances surrounding your life. You may be facing major issues within your marriage, church, job, or life, but let the life of Abram encourage you. God knew exactly what the circumstances looked like for Abram and Sarai. The Lord responded to their circumstances by saying, "This one shall not be your heir, but one who will come from your own body shall be your heir" (Gen. 15:4).

God Keeps His Promises

God has now spoken to Abram three times of the promise given some ten years prior. A son would soon come. God reminded Abram of the promise and ensured that He had not forgotten what He promised. How encouraging this must have been for Abram and Sarai.

Waiting can be so hard. Waiting can cause disappointment to set in as you realize that the promise is not taking place like you thought it would or should. Waiting does not diminish the promise God gives to you. God uses waiting to teach us more about Him and more about being in relationship with Him.

The greatest lesson about trusting in and waiting on the Lord learned took place in Genesis twenty-one; it was then that God gave them their new names, as well. "For Sarah conceived and bore Abraham a son in his old age, at the set time of which God had spoken to him" (Gen 21:2). Abraham learned that God keeps His promises. For the remainder of Abraham's life, he could look back and be reminded that God came through before, and no doubt it encouraged him about the future. If God did it before, then He can do it again.

A Moment of Wonder

I can still feel the deep devastation when I think about a diagnosis I received at eighteen years old. I had graduated from high school and just accepted my first major ministry position as a youth pastor in a church. I was thrilled about what God was doing in my life, and I was excited to also be starting college. I have worn glasses for as long as I can remember, and like many, I go to the eye doctor every year for a checkup. A few weeks after starting college I went for my yearly eye-exam and received the shock of my young life. After the normal exam, my eye doctor asked me to meet her in her office. When we sat down, I could tell something was wrong because she would hardly look at me. She told me, "Matt, I am very sorry to tell you this, but you are going blind."

It was hard to hear anything she said after that first sentence. She tried to explain what she saw and what her expert opinion was regarding my condition. I remember walking down the steps of her office and getting in my truck to drive home. The weight of what I just heard hit me halfway home and I burst into tears. I have no idea how I got home safely because of the tears streaming from my eyes. I remember yelling, "God why? God what are You doing? How could this be part of Your plan?"

At that time, I had been preaching for five years and again had just taken a step in ministry I knew the Lord called me to. I asked the Lord how a blind kid could do all that God had called me to do. None of it made sense to me. When I arrived home, and walked in the door, my mother saw me and immediately knew something terrible happened. With a broken voice I told her and my father what the doctor explained to me. They were devastated. It was one of the hardest days of my life.

The following Wednesday night, I attended my home church and shared with my church family what I was facing. Like a great church family, they gathered around me and anointed me with oil as James five tells us to do. I remember the prayer being simple. I could hear my pastor praying, "God, we have heard what the doctor has said, but Lord we choose to believe Your Word. Your Word says, "...by His stripes we are healed" (Is. 53:5). The prayer ended and the service continued.

My eye doctor scheduled more tests to see if anything could be done to reverse the obvious issue. The day came for me to travel to have a second doctor run tests and that doctor did countless exams and spent half a day working with me. At the conclusion, he met with me and said, "Mr. Turner, I see what your file from your doctor says, but when I look into your eyes, I do not see a thing wrong with them." I burst into tears as I was overwhelmed with gratitude for what God did. While some may try and say that the first doctor made a mistake, I can never be convinced of anything but this: God healed my eyes. Circumstances seemed dark, but that did not matter to the Lord. The circumstances only seemed dark to me; the Lord knew what He was going to do. The Lord touched me and turned my circumstances around.

God can and will do the same in your life as well. Beloved, God never changes. This is one reason why you can rely on the promises He gives. The Lord declared, "For I am the Lord, I do not change" (Mal. 3:6). He also cannot lie. I don't mean He doesn't like to lie; I mean He cannot lie. "God is not a man, that He should lie, Nor a son of man, that He should repent. Has He said, and will He not do?" (Num. 23:19).

Beloved, do not allow the enemy to try and convince you that your circumstances are too big and too problematic. Do no believe the lie of Satan that because it has not happened, it will never happen. No, just one touch or one word from the Lord and everything can change. The Lord does not see the issues you and I face from our perspective; He sees from His perspective, and He sees the beginning and the end.

Abram was given an incredible promise from the Lord and Isaac would soon come. When God told Abram that Eliezer would not be his heir, but that a son would come from him and Sarai, it amazed him that a child could be born from them because of their advanced ages. Abram would never forget—nor would the People of God—what God was about to do in Abram's vision.

Chapter 5 – A Deeper Look

How have you dealt with waiting in the past?

_____

_____

_____

_____

_____

_____

_____

What circumstances have seemed too big to be overcome in your life?

_____

_____

_____

_____

_____

_____

_____

Can you find any specific Scripture that deals with the circumstances you listed above?

_____

_____

_____

_____

_____

_____

When did God prove to you that He is able to do anything, no matter what?

_____

_____

_____

_____

_____

_____

_____

Chapter 6

Step Outside of Distractions

"Then He brought him outside and said, 'Look now toward heaven, and count the stars if you are able to number them.' And He said to him, 'So shall your descendants be.'"
(Genesis 15:5, emphasis added).

Distractions occur every day and sometimes they come in droves. I spend a great deal of time working on projects on my computer through the week. I am constantly writing sermons, designing images for my department's latest ministry resources, responding to emails, managing our social media accounts, and more. Often, there is more work to be done than there are hours in a day. The work is exacerbated daily by distractions. Phone calls, text messages, emails, new projects, and my own personal social media cause some simple tasks to take way longer to complete than they should.

Step Outside of Distractions

Have you ever picked up your phone to open your favorite social media platform and fifteen minutes whiz by before you even realize it? Social media is a deep black hole for time. While I am writing this, I am wondering how many times I pick up my phone and check my social media to see what pops up. To be honest, I might be embarrassed to know. It is a habit I am sad to confess. I am grateful the Lord is still working on me. While social media or whatever distracts you is not bad in itself, often these distractions pull us away from focusing on what we are trying to accomplish. Beloved, there is nothing more important in your life than spending time with God. I do not mean time with God in a church service, or in a prayer meeting, or at a Christian concert. Those things are great, but you and I must have time ALONE with the Lord, time when it is just us and Him. We need it to know God's will for our ministry, our families, and our whole lives.

When the Lord spoke to Abram this third time, God knew something about Abram in the moment. Abram was distracted. Abram did not have social media or 24-hour news to help him be distracted, but he had issues of his own that interfered with the communion he had with God; the distractions made it difficult to hear what the Lord was saying. Abram's distractions were his frustration. He was frustrated with the Lord, he was frustrated with his home life, he was frustrated about his legacy. So when the Lord came to him in Genesis fifteen and spoke of an exceedingly great reward, all Abram could see and focus on was how the promise had not yet come to pass. I am not blaming Abram or pointing my finger. I have been in situations where my circumstances and situation caused me to be distracted from being able to commune with the Lord in prayer and study. The enemy will do anything to keep us from being in the presence of God. The enemy even tried to distract Jesus in the New Testament.

Jesus' ministry began with an incredible jaw-dropping pronouncement from the voice of the Lord. As Jesus came out of the water after being baptized by His cousin John, the Lord spoke, "This is My beloved Son, in whom I am well pleased" (Matt. 3:17). Can you imagine what that must have been like? Wow! From His baptism, Jesus journeys into the Judean desert and spends forty days in fasting and prayer. Our beloved Savior chose to come to this world and suffer and die for all of mankind. Most importantly, He not only knew He would suffer a horrific death, but He also knew He would be raised to life after three days in the grave. The weight of such a purpose must have been terribly heavy. The weight is clearly seen in Christ's time alone in the garden of Gethsemane. The Bible says, "And being in agony, He prayed more earnestly. Then His sweat became like great drops of blood falling down to the ground" (Lk. 22:44). Christ also knew at the beginning of His ministry that He would encounter people with all kinds of sicknesses, diseases, those possessed with devils, and the oppressed. In order to be spiritually prepared to work in this type of ministry, Jesus had to cut His distractions down and get alone with the Lord in prayer and fasting. In fact, while instructing His disciples about casting out demons from one who was full of demons, Jesus told them, "This kind does not go out except by prayer and fasting" (Matt. 17:21).

Jesus knew fasting was— and still is today—a powerful tool that grabs the heart of the Lord to intervene. Fasting helps empty ourselves of distractions so we can be filled with all that God has for us. Toward the end of the fast, the enemy came to Christ to distract and tempt Him.

Satan arrived and appealed to the physical hunger Jesus must have been experiencing. I have never engaged in a complete fast for forty days, however, fasting is an important part of my ministry. I cannot imagine what a person's body would feel like and the hunger one would experience from a fast like the one Jesus completed. No doubt Jesus was weak in body, but His spirit was encouraged and powerful from His time focusing on His Father. Jesus rebukes the enemy with the Word of God by saying, "It is written, 'Man shall not live by bread alone, but by every word that proceeds from the mouth of God'" (Matt. 4:4). Two more times Satan tried to tempt or distract Jesus, but every time, Jesus rebuked him with Scripture.

I shudder to think about what would have happened if Christ had given in to the distractions, even though that was not possible. Christ showed us that it is through Him and God's Word we have the power to overcome the temptations and distractions the enemy tries to throw in our way. He also shows us there is nothing worth deviating from the plan and purpose that God has for us.

Our relationship with God is paramount, and we must be vigilant and guard our quiet times with Him. Turn off our phones, close our doors, turn off the television, lock the kids in their rooms if you have to. Maybe not that last one, but you understand what I am saying. Do whatever it takes to minimize the distractions so you can be alone with God. As the Lord was speaking to Abram in Genesis fifteen, He told Abram to "step outside." This is fascinating to me. Step outside of what? What is going on in this dream or vision that Abram was having that made God change the scenery? The reason God brought Abram "outside" was not only that He had something to show him, but also because of the distractions around him.

God Wants Your Undivided Attention

I have been married for thirteen years to my teenage sweetheart. To say that God blessed me with the most beautiful, intelligent, godly woman I have ever met barely begins to describe how I feel about my wife. I know, and everyone else knows, I married up. After more than a decade of being married, I have learned a few things that get on Anna Kate's nerves more than anything, like chewing. No, I am serious; chewing something crunchy, like cereal or nuts, nearly drives her crazy. Have you thought about the sound of someone chewing? If you are like me, it has never crossed your mind, but my beautiful bride cannot stand that sound. Another thing that drives her crazy is when she is talking to me but I have my phone in my hand and I am distracted, half-listening to her and half-paying attention to whatever is on my phone. I can't say I blame her for this one. I totally understand, and I try my best to give my wife my full attention. Of course, when the roles are reversed, and I am talking to my wife about something I want her to listen to me and for her to have a conversation with me. The Lord is no different. God wants our undivided attention. God has a great deal to tell us. He desires to encourage us, challenge us, and direct us. When we are distracted we have a hard time hearing and receiving anything from the Lord.

Think about this for a moment: God holds your whole life in the palms of His hands. The Lord says, "See, I have inscribed you on the palms of My hands" (Is. 49:16). David said that anywhere he may venture, "Even there Your hand shall lead me, And Your right hand shall hold me" (Ps. 139:10). God knows everything that has happened in our lives and He also knows everything about our tomorrow. Not only does He know what will take place, but He knows what you should do. God has all the answers to every question we could ever ask or encounter. Why would we not give God our full attention? When people ask me, "How can I know what to do in my life?" I always begin by asking them how much time they spend alone with God, reading His word, in prayer, in worship. How much time? A great many Christians go to church once or twice a week and they never think about God from Sunday to Sunday. According to a recent survey by Lifeway Research, only 44% of Protestant churchgoers spend time alone with God on a daily basis.[9] Seventeen percent said they spend time alone with God a few times a week, and 5% say a few times a month.[10] This means that more than half of Protestant churchgoers live their lives without a daily time with the One who not only created the world but who created every life. When we fail to give God our undivided attention, we spiritually tie our hands behind our backs.

How can we know what God desires for our lives when we don't ask and wait for an answer? How can you hear His voice when the only voices you listen to are the myriad voices from reels, from social media? Beloved, God wants to speak to you! God desires to answer your questions, give you peace of mind, and direct your steps in ministry. And like He did in the life of Abram, God desires to fill you with wonder.

Get Alone and Shut the Door

When God brought Abram outside in Genesis fifteen, I thought, *outside of what?* Where was Abram in

---

[9] https://www.christianitytoday.com/news/2023/january/daily-quiet-time-god-prayer-bible-reading-lifeway-survey.html
[10] Ibid.

this vision? Scripture does not ay, but I believe we can look again at the conversation between Abram and God and get an understanding. We know that Abram was somewhere that obstructed the view of the heavens. As we will discuss in the next chapter, God brings Abram outside then lifts up his head to gaze at the stars. So he was inside somewhere. When the word of God came to Abram, he responded by talking about himself and those in his household. It seems that in this vision Abram is around the circumstances that are reminding him of his frustrations. In this vision he perhaps is in his tent or home. In the tent is Sarai, who has not been able to conceive. In the tent is Eliezer, whom Abram mentions to the Lord and perhaps even pointed to as he said, "…one born in my house is my heir" (Gen 15:3). All around Abram were the very things and people that reminded him of what had not gone right in his own sight.

At least in this moment, when Abram sees his wife he is reminded that he has no son. When he looks at Eliezer, he is reminded the promise of a son has not come to pass yet. When he is inside his tent, he is reminded that he is getting older every day and chances are getting slimmer that a son could come. God knew that there was no way Abram would receive a word from the Lord with all those reminders around him. God knew it would be impossible to encourage Abram when he was distracted. Therefore God, "brought him outside."

There is a New Testament teaching from Jesus that shows again that God desires us to get away from distractions so we can have our undivided attention on the Lord, and so we can clearly hear from Him. Jesus, in His famous Sermon on the Mount, begins teaching about prayer in Matthew six. He instructs us, "...when you pray, go into your room, and when you have shut your door, pray to your Father who is in the secret place; and your Father who sees in secret will reward you openly" (Matt. 6:6). In the context of the sermon, Jesus is warning His followers to not be like the religious leaders of the day who were seeking attention by praying in the market and on the streets. Jesus teaches us to abstain from the temptation to "show off" our commitment to prayer, for He assures us that those who seek rewards from men will not receive any from God. Inside the teaching to abstain from prideful prayer is also a very practical lesson; Jesus said, "go into your room, and shut the door." Christ speaks very plainly and to the point: GET ALONE WITH GOD! Leave all distractions in another room, another place, and get alone with the Lord. God knew that Abram couldn't receive His message from inside his tent with all the distractions around him. Jesus knew that you and I have myriad distractions around us, so He told us to get alone and shut the door behind us and pray.

There are plenty of examples through the Old and New Testaments that show us the importance of getting alone with the Lord. Abram's son Isaac got alone in a field to pray and focus on the Lord (Gen.

24:63). In the book of Acts, Peter got on top of a house to get alone and pray (Acts 10:9). Over and over, Jesus got alone, even away from the men He hand-picked to follow Him. We have already talked in this chapter about one time Jesus got alone with God when He journeyed into the wilderness and fasted for forty days. There are at least five other times Jesus slipped away by Himself to pray and talk to the Lord.

There is no way I could over stress to you the value of your time alone with God. Let me encourage you right now, if you have not spent time with God today in prayer and in His Word, when you finish this book, pick up the Book that WILL change your life, the Holy Bible, and read it. Follow up your time in the Word with prayer. If you are not sure what to pray, then start like Jesus started in Matthew six: thank the Lord for being so good and holy. Start telling the Lord how much you love Him and thank Him for saving your life. If you will just start, God will meet you and will begin to speak to you. Don't forget, put your phone up, turn off the TV, and shut your door.

Be Prepared for Interference

There is one thing for sure. When you begin to seek the Lord, Satan cannot stand it. He hates when people begin to call on the name of the Lord. The enemy will do anything and everything possible to stop or delay your time with God.

My wife and I were needing to make some decisions a while back and needed to know the will of God. We decided we were going to take a weekend to fast and pray together. We worked out how we were going to spend time in prayer with three kids. One would keep the kids for thirty minutes while the other went into the bedroom alone to pray. Then we would swap places. The day came for our fast to start, and I was cleaning up our bedroom and moving some books, and somehow, while moving those books, I slipped a disk in my back. While I have dealt with this type of injury before, this time was the absolute worst. I could hardly move and when I did it was very painful. If you have ever experienced something like this, then you understand completely. Some might ask, "What does your hurt back have to do with fasting?" You cannot convince me of anything but this: the enemy knew my wife and I were planning on fasting. He heard us talking about it and how we were getting excited about hearing from God, and he could not stand it. While the enemy thought he would keep me from fasting, he was terribly mistaken. I fasted that weekend just like I planned. Now, I had to fast from the floor, as that was the only way I could get some relief. While fasting that week, God sent a peace to our hearts and minds about what we were praying about and we received the answer we sought God about.

God will never fail us. He desires to speak to us. Jesus said, "Ask, and it will be given to you; seek, and you will find; knock, and it will be opened to you" (Matt. 7:7).

Now, please hear me: I am not saying that every time you decide to spend time with the Lord the enemy is going to come attack your body. I am saying Satan cannot stand you talking to God the Father. He will do anything in his limited power to stop it. As a result, he will try to bring interference into your life. He will devise some new distraction to come up right as you sat down to read God's Word or pray. He will try his best to stop you. Beware of his tactics. Expect him to try and distract you. Then you will recognize the phone call, text message, tv show or whatever for what it is, a distraction. You will then be able to say, *I do not have to respond right at this minute.* It can wait fifteen minutes so you can spend a little time in prayer talking to the One who loves you.

A Moment of Wonder

Getting alone with God is crucial to our relationship with Him. Imagine being married to your spouse but never going home to spend time with them. That would not be much of a relationship. God desires to be more than an acquaintance. In fact, God demands through His Word that we place Him in the top spot of importance in our lives. Christ commanded, "You shall love the Lord your God with all your heart and with all your soul and with all your mind" (Matt. 22:37). There is no other option. In the book of Revelation, God says He gets sick to his stomach over those who are half serious about a relationship with Him. God told the church of the Laodiceans, "…because you are lukewarm, and neither cold nor hot, I will vomit you out of My mouth" (Rev. 3:16). However, for those who will focus on Christ and spend time with Him, God will not only guide and direct them, but bless them abundantly.

While finishing this book, my wife and I started a twenty-one day Daniel's Fast© [11] along with our home church. In the book of Daniel (1:8-14), Daniel and his companions decided they would not eat the choice food, meats, cheeses, sweets, from the king's table in order to keep his Jewish tenets of faith. Those around him thought Daniel was crazy, but Daniel was confident that God would sustain him through his period of fasting. At the end of the fast, Scripture says that he and others who joined in with Daniel, "…appeared better and fatter in flesh than all the young men who ate the portion of the king's delicacies" (Dan. 1:15). God honored Daniel because of his fasting and his trust in the Lord.

Many people in the Christian world, especially the Pentecostal faith, participate in a Daniel's fast every year. As I mentioned, my wife and I started a Daniel's fast as I was getting close to finishing the manuscript of *Count the Stars*. A few months prior, I submitted a few inquiries to publishers just to see if by chance any company was interested. If you look up the stats, it is amazing that only one to three percent of authors get published. My previous two works, *Follow Him©* and

---

[11] https://www.biblestudytools.com/bible-study/topical-studies/whats-the-daniel-fast-and-how-do-you-do-it.html

Step Outside of Distractions

Discipleship Journey©, I self-published, which was such a blessing, but it was a huge prayer of mine—as I am sure it is of any author—for a company to not only see value in me as an author, but more important, to see the value and ministry of what I have written.

Half-way through my time of fasting and prayer, I received word from Kharis Publishing® that they were interested in acquiring *Count the Stars*. I was and still am blown away at the gift God has given me and my family by putting Kharis in my path. I absolutely believe that because I have spent time seeking God, desiring to get closer to Him, cutting out distractions, saying no to things that waste time, so I could spend time with Christ, God has blessed me. Truthfully, there are many other things God has done as a result of the fast but bringing a publisher for *Count the Stars* is something that causes me to stand in awe and wonder of our great God.

Chapter 6 – A Deeper Look

What is your biggest distraction when you try to pray or study God's Word?

_____

_____

_____

_____

_____

_____

Do you think God deserves your undivided attention? If so, what can you do to help you totally focus on Him?

_____

_____

_____

_____

_____

_____

_____

Have you ever had the enemy try and distract you or cause something to happen to keep you from spending time with God? What happened?

_____

_____

_____

_____

_____

_____

Think back and write down a time where God blew your mind with a blessing?

_____

_____

_____

_____

_____

_____

_____

_____

Chapter 7

An Impossible Task

> *Then He brought him outside and said, "Look now toward heaven, and count the stars if you are able to number them." And He said to him, "So shall your descendants be."*
> (Genesis 15:5, emphasis added).

I would have loved to have been in the moment when God brought Abram outside to gaze into the heavens. So much has already happened in this conversation, as we have discussed in detail, but verse five is a powerful and beautiful moment. It could only be eclipsed by what is described in the next verse, which we will talk about in the conclusion of this book.

The story and the circumstances surrounding this conversation drastically changes after Abram steps outside. The conversation that was filled with such frustration and disappointment not only changes, but all those feelings that Abram has been honest about begin to melt. In verse five, Abram walks outside full of pain and carrying the weight of trying to figure out what to do. By the end of verse five, Abram's whole life changes. The anger, fear and frustration Abram that harbored in his life are replaced by peace, hope, and wonder.

The process that God uses to change Abram's life is, in my opinion, somewhat unorthodox. What I mean by that is, I am not sure anyone would have thought that what God did and asked of Abram was a good idea. I am not sure anyone would think what God did would make anything better. In his own summation, Abram was faced with an impossible situation. Trying to conceive and bring an heir into the world seemed impossible. Years had gone by, even with a promise from the Lord. It seemed impossible. God's answer to this situation to help Abram with his frustration in Genesis fifteen was not to bring Isaac into the world right then. No, God asked Abram to do something that absolutely was impossible for Abram to accomplish. God asked Abram to try to count the stars he saw in the night sky. Absolutely impossible. But before we discus that, lets dive into what happened as Abram steps outside.

Notice Abram's Posture

When God brings Abram outside his tent, as we discussed in the last chapter and are reviewing here, God tells him to look up into the heavens. It gives us this picture that when Abram walked outside his head was hanging down as if he walked outside in discouragement. In verse four, God for the third time tells Abram that a son, a natural blood son, would be coming. But let's be honest, Abram has heard this twice before. Please don't misunderstand what I am saying, I am not suggesting that God's word to Abram was less miraculous or powerful because He said it before. I am trying to put us in the shoes of Abram as far as that might be possible.

Abram has heard the promise of the Lord before. He has been holding on to the promise of a son for some ten years by this point. God telling Abram to lift his head is not hard to understand. Abram has been through a lot, and he is having a hard day with his faith. You can understand where Abram is, right? We all have days when we feel like it's hard to raise our heads. We love the Lord, we trust the Lord, but some days are harder than others. No doubt, at times the enemy comes and whispers lies in our minds and those lies sometimes take root; their fruits are fear, doubt, and worry. Then somedays are just filled with life, and life can be tough. No matter the source, we all have hard days.

While I was writing this chapter, I was barricaded in my room away from my family because I was sick with COVID-19. I praise the Lord that my experience this time has been much like the last several times; symptoms have been mostly mild, but I remember, as I'm sure you do, what it was like in 2020. As we heard of COVID-19 spreading across the nation, the first person I was close to that contracted the sickness was my friend and my employer. When I first heard that he was ill and had tested positive, while I knew it was serious, I never expected the worst to happen. However, in just a few short weeks he went home to be with the Lord.

Being an overseer of the church in the United States, I kept up with our pastors, ministers, and their families who not only became sick, but those who succumbed. It was heartbreaking. I remember dealing with all the reports at work, only to come home to watch the news for the remainder of the night seeing the latest news from around the country. It was hard. It was difficult for everyone. The whole world was dealing with the effects of the disease.

During that time, I found myself living my life with my head hanging down. Many were experiencing the same, as well. We went to work with our heads hanging down, we went home with our heads down, we went to church with our heads down. Our lives were consumed by this disease in many ways.

While the situations are nothing alike, my situation helps me to understand what Abram might have been feeling. He was just overwhelmed with the desire to have a son. God told him for a third time that a son would soon come. When Abram walked outside, he didn't feel like lifting his head. Have you ever been at a place like this where life hits hard? Sometimes it feels like we get knocked down and before we can get back up, we are hit with another issue. Because of all of this, many times we feel like we do not have the strength to lift up our heads. Beloved, if that is you today, there is good news. You may not have the strength, but our God does.

Be encouraged today that when you are weak, God will not sit idly by and not intervene. Isaiah tells us a wonderful truth about our God: "He gives power to the weak, And to those who have no might He increases strength" (Is. 40:29). Our God does not lack in power and might, as we have previously discussed. His ability goes beyond all comprehension. When you call upon Him as a loving Father who comes to the aid of a child, so God will stretch out His mighty hand to strengthen you. As Isaiah says, our Father gives power to the weak. Are you weak today? Can I encourage you that you are in the perfect spot to receive power from the Lord? The enemy may be thinking that he has you right where he wants you to strike the final blow, but the Lord has been aware of your situation all this time, and power is on its way.

Do you feel like all of your strength has been depleted? The enemy loves to tempt those who are weak, and try to cause them to stray from the Lord. However, we have been given a promise from the Lord that it is in the times of weakness, when we feel as though we are empty of might, that the Lord sends strength. Beloved, do not allow yourself to doubt for one second. God is still on your side and strength is coming. Power is on its way. Hold on; God will come through for you.

There is a verse of Scripture that I quote to myself all the time. The Lord speaks to the Prophet Jeremiah and says, "Call to Me, and I will answer you, and show you great and mighty things, which you do not know" (Jeremiah 33:3). God gives Jeremiah, and us today, a promise. If we call out to Him, He will not be able to ignore our cry. While there are over eight billion people in this world today, when we call on the Lord, He comes right where we are to intervene on our behalf.[12]

So, beloved, lift up your head. As the Psalmist said, let us "…lift up my eyes to the hills from whence comes my help? My help comes from the Lord, who made heaven and earth" (Ps. 121:1-2). When the Lord brought Abram outside of the tent, I believe that while Abram was discouraged and frustrated with his circumstances, the Spirit of God strengthened him in this moment to lift his head. When Abram set his eyes on the night sky, I believe everything changed in Abram's mind. It was a moment that marked him. He never forgot the night he lifted his head and was filled with wonder.

Be Filled with the Wonder of the Creator

When Abram lifted up his head, he was confronted with the undeniable creative ability of the Lord. As Abram gazed into the heavens, he saw, as you and I do, an array of bright dots in the midst of a black void that is space. He saw differences in the stars. They were

---

[12] https://www.census.gov/popclock/

different colors, they seemingly twinkled, and some appeared larger than others. I believe the Lord wanted to show Abram that He was, and still is today, a master creator. Scripture declares, "Then God made two great lights: the greater light to rule the day, and the lesser light to rule the night. He made the stars also. God set them in the firmament of the heavens to give light on the earth" (Gen. 1:16-17). I love how Moses describes the moment in time when God created the stars in the sky. Five words mark the event. "He made the stars also", Moses said. I suppose our minds could not comprehend the information needed to explain the specifics of how God made the stars and how He made them is not the important point. The important fact to know is that God made them. The stars are there in the night sky because the Lord made them.

According to NASA, "Astronomers estimate that the universe could contain up to one septillion stars — that's a one followed by 24 zeros. Our Milky Way alone contains more than 100 billion, including our most well-studied star, the Sun."[13] When the Lord drew Abram's attention to the heavens, He must have been astounded and humbled as he viewed the handy work of the Lord. What was the point of God showing Abram all those stars? One reason was so Abram would know that since the Lord created all the stars in the sky, then surely he can create and give a son to Abram and Sarai. In other words, God showed Abram

---

[13] https://science.nasa.gov/universe/stars/

that nothing was too hard for Him. There is nothing outside the realm of possibilities with God. His might is unmatched, His creativity is unending, and His ability exceeds all understanding.

The creativity of the Lord is seen throughout scripture. Moses, who wrote the account of Abram, knew well how creative God was. As the Lord led the Children of Israel out of Egypt, He provided food for them every day. The Lord said, "I will rain down bread from heaven for you. The people are to go out each day and gather enough for that day. In this way I will test them and see whether they will follow my instructions. On the sixth day they are to prepare what they bring in, and that is to be twice as much as they gather on the other days" (Ex. 16:4-5). When the people of God complained about not having meat to eat, the Lord sent quail. Moses recorded, "That evening quail came and covered the camp" (Ex. 16:13). When the people of God had any need, the Lord provided. He created and sent manna to sustain them. He sent quail to satisfy them. Water flowed from a rock to quench their thirst (Ex 17:6). Over and over the creativity of the Lord can be seen.

In the New Testament, God was still a creative God. In Matthew fourteen, Jesus took five loaves of bread and two fishes and fed thousands of people. The details of the creative miracle are not recorded. However, that is not the important point. The fact that God did it is the most important point.

You may be reading this and are in a place where you need the Lord to work a creative miracle in your life. Maybe the bills are piling up, your family is struggling to eat, or the doctors have not given you much hope. I want to encourage you to lift up your head and look at the stars in the night sky. If the Lord can create what is seen and what is not seen, then surely, He can create a miracle for you.

This was the message to Abram. While a son had not yet come, it did not mean God had run out of creative power. I believe God wanted to fill Abram's mind with wonder that no doubt stayed with him for the rest of his life. He stood in awe of the creative might of God. That day, in Genesis fifteen, Abram was encouraged as he looked into the heavens, that God could indeed bring a son into the world as He promised.

Be Filled with the Wonder of the Sustainer

As Abram looked into the sky, not only was he overwhelmed with the creativity of the Lord, but also at how God can sustain all he saw in the heavens. How amazing is it that a star in the sky that is composed of gas, matter, light, and more, continues to burn and light the night sky for thousands and thousands of years? I do not pretend to know much at all about what makes up a star. There are many in the world who are far more knowledgeable about such things than I am. I do know and believe that the God who created the stars is also the One who has kept them there all this time.

An Impossible Task

Becoming a father put a new sense of responsibility in me that is unmatched by anything. As a father, I am responsible for the three gifts God has given me. My two girls and little boy are precious to me. When my first child was born, I was very overprotective. Sometimes, I would sit in her room just watching her to make sure that she was still breathing while she slept. I know, a little over the top. I quickly found out that I could not watch her every second of every day. I had to rest as well. I had to learn that the same God who gave me my beautiful girl was also more than able to sustain her. Every night, I pray over all my kids. We ask the Lord to help us have a better day tomorrow than we did today. We ask for the Lord to keep us safe, and we ask the Lord to help us grow closer to Him. Scripture declares, "The Lord is your keeper" (Ps. 121:5). He is the one who looks over us, sustains us, and works on our behalf, even when we are clueless to His workings.

As Abram looked up into the night sky, he was filled with amazement at the Lord's handiwork. The Psalmist says, "He counts the number of the stars; He calls them all by name" (Ps. 147:4). Now, if the Lord knows all the stars in the sky by name, and He has sustained them for countless years, then surely, He can also take care of you. You are far more valuable to the Lord than the stars in the sky. How do I know? Because God sent His Son Jesus into the world to save you. He did not come to save the stars, trees, or the bears. He came for you. This was the message Abram heard deep down in his spirit. God's ability is unmatched and whatever God creates or does, He also will sustain.

Try to Count the Stars

The Lord told Abram, "Count the stars if you are able to number them" (Gen 15:5). I wonder what Abram's first reaction was to such a thought. We are not told that Abram gave any type of response to God's request. When the Lord draws Abram's attention up to the heavens, He asks Abram to do something that is impossible. It was impossible because Abram could not see all the stars in the sky. As I mentioned earlier, NASA says the heavens "could contain up to one septillion star"[14] Even with today's technology and all the power our modern telescopes have, we still do not know the depths of all God has created. Scripture does not share any detail between verse five and six about any conversation between Abram and God after the Lord asked Abram to count the stars. However, I believe that it went something like this:

> **Abram**: What do you mean you want me to count the stars? What does that have to do with anything?

> **God**: Abram, I know you don't understand. I am trying to help you understand. Look and see if you can number them.

---

[14] https://science.nasa.gov/universe/stars/

Abram: Lord, I am tired, we have talked about Sarai having a child over and over, and I know you keep saying a son is coming, but it seems like it is beyond possible now. Before, I thought maybe it could happen, but now it just seems hopeless.

God: Abram, look up here. Now, count them; tell me how many do you see.

Abram: 1, 2, 3, 4, 5, 6, 7... God this is impossible, I could never do this. How could someone count the stars? There are just too many! It is impossible!

God: This is what I have been trying to get you to see.

Abram: You have been trying to get me to see having a child is impossible like numbering the stars is impossible?

God: No, beloved, I know you cannot count the stars, but I can. I know you think counting the stars in the sky is impossible, but I am the One who placed them there. I know you cannot understand how the stars are held in place, but I am the One who holds them there. I know you do not know how a child can be born after all these years, but I do. Even though you cannot, I can.

Of course, Scripture does not record any such interaction between Abram and the Lord, but no doubt

God desired to show Abram that since He could create the stars in the sky, He surely could bring a son into the world. I believe when Abram lifted up his head and saw the innumerable stars in the sky, he realized that there truly is nothing too hard for the Lord. In fact, God asserted to Abram and to all of humanity that nothing is too hard for Him. "Is anything too hard for the Lord? At the appointed time I will return to you, according to the time of life, and Sarah shall have a son" (Gen. 18:14). Because of our limited power and ability, there are countless things that are too hard for me and you. Our God is not limited by anything.

When Paul wrote the book of Ephesians, he tried to find the right words to describe the ability of the Lord. He struggled for just one word so he used four. "Now to Him who is able to do exceedingly abundantly above all that we ask or think, according to the power that works in us" (Eph. 3:20). Exceedingly. Abundantly. Above All.

In her book, *God Is Able*©, Priscilla Shirer challenges her readers to think about what it would take to completely change a situation you are facing that causes you to fear or worry. What drastic turnaround would have to happen for the issue you might be facing today to not only go away, but also to leave you in a better position than before the problem arose. Now that you have that in your mind, Shirer encourages us all by sharing, "He (God) can go beyond that!"[15] In other words, whatever you can think of, God can do more than that! There is nothing He cannot do, nothing. This is what God was trying to share with Abram as He told him to lift his head to the sky. Beloved, be encouraged today that God can do anything; just look up and try to count the stars.

A Moment of Wonder

As we have discussed, when you are in the middle of a crisis it is hard to lift up your head. It is hard to see anything but the problem you are facing. To combat this, use the Word of God. Remind yourself of God's amazing ability to turn situations around.

In 2010, I became the Senior Pastor of the Piedmont Congregational Holiness Church in northeast Alabama. I had just turned twenty-two years old, and I had no idea what I was doing. I did know I heard the voice of the Lord to take the step of faith and pastor the wonderful people of Piedmont. One of the precious people who made a lasting impact on my life was a Sunday school teacher named Judy Freeman. Mrs. Judy was a woman of faith who loved the Lord. I remember one particular series she taught on faith and healing. She shared that while dealing with a terrible sickness herself, she wrote on index cards every healing verse she could find in the Bible. Then, every morning and evening, as if she was taking medicine to combat

---

[15] Priscilla Shire, God Is Able (Nashville, B&H Publishing, 2013) 80.

the sickness, she would read those index cards full of God's Word. She soon began to get better and the ailment that she suffered soon was healed. She challenged us in her class to do the same. I have never forgotten that exercise, and I now challenge you. Are you facing sickness, disease, worry, fear, or anything else? Get into the Word of God and began to "take" the scriptures as you would a medicine from a physician. Allow God's Word to get down in your heart and spirit. Let the discipline of reading God's word become a daily practice. Where should you start? I am glad you asked.

Three of God's Truths to Speak Over Your Life

1) **God Is Strength.** Remember who is on your side. God is strength and He lives in you! After crossing the Red Sea, Moses and the Children of Israel sang, "The Lord is my strength and song, And He has become my salvation" (Ex 15:2). Can you imagine what it must have been like to cross the Red Sea on dry ground? Or see the enemy of Israel, Pharaoh and his army, drowned in the sea? If God can do all of that, what can he do in our lives today?

2) **I Can Rely on His Strength.** It is wonderful to know God has the power to split seas, but it is another thing to know God gives you strength. Paul said, "Finally, my brethren, be strong in the Lord and in the power of His might" (Eph. 6:10). Life can take all our strength from us, but. we can rely on God's strength. In the history of the world,

God has never lost a battle. When Christ died, while the enemy of our soul thought he had finally killed the Lord, he was sorely mistaken. Christ arose from the grave with victory, and we walk in that victory every day because He lives in our hearts. You can rest at night knowing that He will keep you.

3) **God Can Do Anything.** While it is hard to wrap our minds around the idea that there is nothing that hinders God nor His ability, it does not change the facts. God can do anything. God proved in the beginning, the mere command of His voice caused matter to appear, mountains to rise, and oceans to split. "Then God said, 'Let there be light'; and there was light" (Gen 1:3). God speaks and things happen.

Chapter 7 - A Deeper Look

When have you felt like Abram, and been unable to lift your head? How did the Lord help you through that time?

_____

_____

_____

_____

_____

_____

Has the Lord ever created an answer to your situation that blew your mind?

_____

_____

_____

_____

_____

_____

_____

Share a time where you learned that God is a sustainer.

_____

_____

_____

_____

_____

_____

_____

What are some of your favorite verses in the Bible that you could use every day?

_____

_____

_____

_____

_____

_____

_____

_____

Conclusion

I remember sitting in my home church in Griffin, GA as the pastor read Genesis 15:1-6 as a reference for a sermon he was preaching one particular Sunday morning. I have heard and read the story of Abram countless times, but this time something different happened. I felt the Lord prick my heart to spend some time studying the early life of Abram. I thought it would just be a sermon I would preach about the hope and power of the Lord. The Lord indeed helped me to preach a few messages from this great passage of Scripture, but the Lord continued to deal with me about these verses as I felt there was more for me to learn. I am grateful that God's word is an endless fountain from which we all can draw knowledge and strength. The story of Abram particularly is full of the wonder of God. Oh, I would have loved to have been there when God asked Abram to look up into the heavens. It must have been so powerful and inspiring. This one moment changed the life of Abram. At the conclusion of verse five, the very next verse simply states, "And he believed in the Lord…" (Gen. 15:6).

Conclusion

Abram Was Fully Convinced

The conversation that took place over Genesis fifteen verses one through five was so powerful that by the end of a short discourse Abram's frustration not only dissipated, but Abram was fully convinced in the sovereignty of the Lord. He decided that he was going to believe everything the Lord told him. Genesis 15:6 was the day that Abram would forever look back at and remember it was the day he chose to believe and trust the Lord. Abram never regretted that day.

Did Abram ever make another mistake? He absolutely did. In fact, in the next chapter Abram and Sarai try to "help" the Lord bring the promised son into the world. Sarai gave her maid Hagar to Abram and the result of that relationship was Ishmael coming into the world. While no life is a mistake, Abram and Sari's actions were not the will of the Lord. Abram was not perfect, but God loved him and choose him anyways. This is the beautiful truth about the Lord: He loves us in spite of our failures and mistakes.

Abram believed in the Lord. While this is a wonderful and beautiful moment, I do not find it shocking because I have had similar encounters with the Lord. While my story is quite different from Abram's, I too have experienced mighty encounters with the Lord. Those moments over the course of my life have convinced me that God not only exists, but that He loves me and works to bring blessing into my life.

Do you remember the meeting between Jesus and Peter and Andrew in Matthew 4:19? It is a place in the ministry of Jesus that has always blown me away. Because of one sentence spoken by Jesus, Peter and Andrew became convinced to follow Him. Jesus said, "Follow Me, and I will make you fishers of men" (Matt. 4:19). In this one encounter, Jesus changed the lives of two rugged fisherman. This one encounter fully convinced the disciples to alter the direction of their lives. The next verse says, "They immediately left their nets and followed Him" (Matt. 4:20). There was no question in the minds of the disciples who Jesus was and what direction they needed to take.

What about your life? Have you had an interaction with the Lord that has convinced you that the Lord exists and that He desires the best for your life? It is great to think back to those moments in our lives. As hard days come, we can always go back in our minds where we had an encounter with God that changed our lives. Let me encourage you to keep on believing.

Keep On Believing

In an interesting periodical, Max Rogland suggests the use of the verb "believed" in Gen. 15:6, may have the wrong tense. In our English translations, it is translated that when the Lord spoke to Abram that the result of that conversation was Abram's decision to believe the Lord. Rogland does not dispute this completely, rather, he argues that the better translation

Conclusion

is "Abram kept believing God."[16] Do you see the difference? From Rogland's point of view, Abram did not just believe the Lord in one place in one moment in his life, but rather over and over choose to believe the Lord. I love this thought. I love it because this is what you and I do throughout our lives.

Do we not choose to believe the Lord every time we are faced with a temptation? When we say no to a temptation, we are saying that we believe the Lord and what His Word says. When we pray for those who are sick and ask the Lord to heal our family and friends, are we not choosing to believe the Lord again by trusting in His Word that says, "…by His stripes we are healed" (Is. 53:5)? Our trust in the Lord, while it starts in a single moment the day we received Christ as our Savior, like Abram, we continue to choose to believe the Lord. Rogland continues by saying, "Abram's believing in the Lord is not to be viewed as a single moment of trust that took place in Gen. 15 but rather as something that occurred repeatedly."[17]

Beloved, let me encourage you to continue, every day, to believe in the Lord. Today is a day you must choose. Will you believe the report of man or the report

---

[16] Rogland, Max Frederick. 2008. "Abram's Persistent Faith: Hebrew Verb Semantics in Genesis 15:6." *The Westminster Theological Journal* 70 (2): 239–44.

https://search.ebscohost.com/login.aspx?direct=true&AuthTyp e=sso&db=lsdar&AN=ATLA0001700958&authtype=shib&site =eds-live&scope=site.

[17] Ibid.

of the Lord? Joshua said: Now therefore, fear the Lord, serve Him in sincerity and in truth, and put away the gods which your fathers served on the other side of the River and in Egypt. Serve the Lord! And if it seems evil to you to serve the Lord, choose for yourselves this day whom you will serve, whether the gods which your fathers served that were on the other side of the River, or the gods of the Amorites, in whose land you dwell. But as for me and my house, we will serve the Lord" (Josh. 24:14-15).

Decide today to trust and believe in the Lord.
Let me leave you with three things.

Be Open To God

From the moment the Lord first called Abram, his life was full of adventure. Boring is not an adjective that can be used to describe a life with Jesus. God wants to take you on the adventure of a lifetime. Be open to the Lord leading you. What if God called you to leave everything you knew? What if He asked you to leave your hometown and drive across the country to a small town in some state that is completely different from the one you are accustomed to? Would you obey the Lord? My prayer is that you will say yes to Him.

Be Open With God

God knows everything about your life and what is on the inside of your heart, yet He still desires to hear from you. Be open with Him and talk to Him. Share with the Lord your worries, fears, heartaches, and pain.

Conclusion

He can handle it all. You and I were not made to carry the load we so often try to carry: "Casting all your care upon Him, for He cares for you" (1 Pet. 5:7). You do not have to do life by yourself. You can have someone with you who will care for you and help you.

Be Open For God

The Lord desires to use you. While Scripture does not detail every conversation Abram had with others, I believe Abram told everyone he encountered about the Lord. I believe Abram shared how God called him out of Ur and how the Lord delivered him and his wife out of Egypt and blessed them with great wealth. The truth is, when God does something for you, it's harder to keep silent than it is to tell someone. Let me challenge you to tell someone today what God has done for you. Allow the Lord to use you. Be open for the Lord to use you for His glory! There are people all around us who live with their heads hanging down. Tell them about Jesus and how they can lift up their heads and be filled with wonder.

Beloved, I pray that you will never look at a night sky the same. I pray when you see the stars in the sky you will be reminded about Abram and be reminded that God loves you so much. Lift up your eyes and count the stars.

References

Introduction

https://adaa.org/understanding-anxiety/facts-statistics accessed 3/14/2024

He Knows my Name©, 2013, Annie and Kelly McRae, Gospel Lighthouse

Chapter 1

Blenkinsopp, Joseph. 2016. "The First Family: Terah and Sons." *Journal for the Study of the Old Testament* 41 (1): 3–13. https://search-ebscohost-com.seu.idm.oclc.org/login.aspx?direct=true&db=oah&AN=OTA0000067293&site=eds-live&scope=site.

Henry Halley. Halley's Bible Handbook. (Grand Rapids: Zondervan, 1965) 95.

Chapter 3

David Roper, Seeing God: Meet God In the Unexpected (Grand Rapids, MI, Discovery House Publishers, 2006) 102.

Chapter 5

https://biblehub.com/hebrew/2009.htm February 13, 2024

References

Chapter 6

https://www.christianitytoday.com/news/2023/january/daily-quiet-time-god-prayer-bible-reading-lifeway-survey.html, accessed Jan. 4, 2024.

Chapter 7

https://www.census.gov/popclock/, accessed Feb 16, 2024.

https://science.nasa.gov/universe/stars/ accessed Feb 16, 2024.

Priscilla Shire, God Is Able (Nashville, B&H Publishing, 2013) 80.

Conclusion

Rogland, Max Frederick. 2008. "Abram's Persistent Faith: Hebrew Verb Semantics in Genesis 15:6." *The Westminster Theological Journal* 70 (2): 239–44. https://search.ebscohost.com/login.aspx?direct=true&AuthType=sso&db=lsdar&AN=ATLA0001700958&authtype=shib&site=eds-live&scope=site.

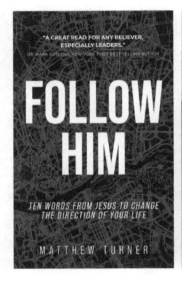
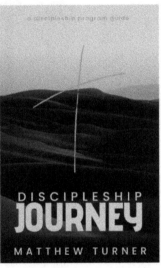

About
Kharis Publishing:

Kharis Publishing, an imprint of Kharis Media LLC, is a leading Christian and inspirational book publisher based in Aurora, Chicago metropolitan area, Illinois. Kharis' dual mission is to give voice to under-represented writers (including women and first-time authors) and equip orphans in developing countries with literacy tools. That is why, for each book sold, the publisher channels some of the proceeds into providing books and computers for orphanages in developing countries so that these kids may learn to read, dream, and grow. For a limited time, Kharis Publishing is accepting unsolicited queries for nonfiction (Christian, self-help, memoirs, business, health and wellness) from qualified leaders, professionals, pastors, and ministers. Learn more at: https://kharispublishing.com/

Printed in the USA
CPSIA information can be obtained
at www.ICGtesting.com
CBHW071643240624
10284CB00004B/14

9 781637 462591